Finished on 5 Dec. 2022

Started on 4 Dec 2022

Wild Problems

A Guide to the Decisions
That Define Us

RUSS ROBERTS

PORTFOLIO | PENGUIN

Portfolio / Penguin
An imprint of Penguin Random House LLC
penguinrandomhouse.com

Most Portfolio books are available at a discount when purchased in quantity for
sales promotions or corporate use. Special editions, which include personalized
covers, excerpts, and corporate imprints, can be created when purchased in large
quantities. For more information, please call (212) 572-2232 or e-mail
specialmarkets@penguinrandomhouse.com. Your local bookstore can also assist
with discounted bulk purchases using the Penguin Random House corporate
Business-to-Business program. For assistance in locating a participating
retailer, e-mail B2B@penguinrandomhouse.com.

LIBRARY OF CONGRESS CATALOGING-IN-PUBLICATION DATA
Names: Roberts, Russell, 1953– author.
Title: Wild problems: a guide to the decisions that define us / Russ Roberts.
Description: First Edition. | New York, NY: Portfolio / Penguin, [2022] |
Includes bibliographical references.
Identifiers: LCCN 2022007224 (print) | LCCN 2022007225 (ebook) |
ISBN 9780593418253 (hardcover) | ISBN 9780593418260 (ebook)
Subjects: LCSH: Decision making.
Classification: LCC BF448 .R636 2022 (print) | LCC BF448 (ebook) |
DDC 153.8/3—dc23/eng/20220527
LC record available at https://lccn.loc.gov/2022007224
LC ebook record available at https://lccn.loc.gov/2022007225

Printed in the United States of America
1   3   5   7   9   10   8   6   4   2

Book design by Jessica Shatan Heslin/Studio Shatan, Inc.

To Sharon

Tastes, smells, the sensations of heat and cold, beauty, pleasure, all the affections and appetites of the mind, wisdom, folly, and most kinds of probability, with many other things too tedious to enumerate, admit of degrees, but have not yet been reduced to measure, nor, as I apprehend, ever can be. . . . Until our affections and appetites shall themselves be reduced to quantity, and exact measures of their various degrees be assigned, in vain shall we essay to measure virtue and merit by them. This is only to ring changes upon words, and to make a show of mathematical reasoning, without advancing one step in real knowledge.

—Thomas Reid, "An Essay on Quantity," 1748

Most of the profoundly important activities, relationships, and forms of knowledge that human beings pursue are ones a person can fully appreciate, and integrate into her value-system, only once she is well acquainted with them.

—Agnes Callard, *Aspiration*

The only thing that makes life possible is permanent, intolerable uncertainty: not knowing what comes next.

—Ursula K. Le Guin, *The Left Hand of Darkness*

Human beings are not born once and for all on the day their mothers give birth to them, but that life obliges them over and over again to give birth to themselves.

—Gabriel García Márquez, *Love in the Time of Cholera*

The need for certainty is the greatest disease the mind faces.

—Robert Greene, *Mastery*

Contents

Wild Problems

1

Wild Problems

A few years ago, a friend and I were out walking, and he told me that he and his wife were struggling with the decision of whether to have a child. He told me they had made a list of the costs and benefits of children, and after having done so, they still weren't sure whether it was a good idea. My friend asked for my advice.

I told him that you don't have a child because it's "worth it." I didn't have much else to tell him. I didn't think to ask him whether he and his wife thought they had any idea of what becoming a parent was really like. Before you have children, the costs you can imagine—less time for work

---

and play, limited vacation options, money spent on diapers, clothes, food, education, and so on—dominate any imaginable benefits.

Having children might then seem irrational. Yet many parents, including myself, will tell you that their children are central to how they see themselves and how they experience life. Many parents would say that having children gives their lives meaning. How can we understand that disconnect?

Whether to have a child is what I call a wild problem—a fork in the road of life where knowing which path is the right one isn't obvious, where the pleasure and pain from choosing one path over another are ultimately hidden from us, where the path we choose defines who we are and who we might become. Wild problems are the big decisions all of us have to deal with as we go through life.

A lot of wild problems can give us butterflies and make our hearts ache. Knowing which path is the best one can't be answered until we arrive in that distant land known as the future, a land we know fully only when we arrive. That tends to unnerve us. Lacking nerve, we procrastinate.

How should we proceed, then, especially if we want to make a rational decision? An obvious strategy is to import help from other challenges we've faced and know how to solve. To beat the traffic or develop a vaccine against the coronavirus, for example, we rely on data, algorithms that can be tested, and experiments that can be replicated. For certain problems—I call them tame problems—the relentless application of science, engineering, and rational thought leads to steady progress.

But the big decisions we face in life, the wild problems—whether to marry, who to marry, whether to have children, what career path to follow, how much time to devote to friends and family, how to resolve daily ethical dilemmas—these big decisions can't be made with data, or science, or the usual rational approaches.

I was trained as an economist at the University of Chicago. We were taught that economics is the guide to making rational choices in life. We were taught the importance of trade-offs and what is called opportunity cost—what we give up when we choose one thing over another. We were taught that everything has a price—everything involves giving up something to have something else. Nothing is of infinite value. I have come to believe that when it comes to the big decisions of life, those principles can lead us astray.

Carved into the wall of the building that houses the

economics department when I was a graduate student at the University of Chicago is a quote from Lord Kelvin: "When you cannot measure, your knowledge is meager and unsatisfactory." The modern world has taken Lord Kelvin to heart. First the sciences, and increasingly the social sciences and even the humanities, have embraced the idea that measuring—collecting data—and improving the process that produces the measurement, and using those measurements to get stronger, more productive, and healthier, is the road to a better life.

But wild problems resist measurement. What works for you might not work for me, and what worked for me yesterday might not work for me tomorrow. Wild problems are untamed, undomesticated, spontaneous, organic, complex. They're a whole different beast compared to the tame problems where the standard techniques of rationality move us steadily forward.

Through most of human history, authority and tradition—the kings who ruled us, our parents, the religion we were born into, the culture surrounding us— tamed the wild problems we faced. The kings are dead. Religion's hold steadily loosens. Tradition? We shuck it off and imagine ourselves as blank slates where we hold the chalk and can draw ourselves the way we'd like to be, free of all constraints.

Tame Problems	Wild Problems
Goals are clear and objectively assessed.	Goals are subjective and hard to measure.
How to get to Chicago from New York	Whether to go to Chicago
Techniques for success can be tested and verified. Recipes work.	There is no manual, road map, recipe, or algorithm for success.
Making an omelet	Writing *Hamlet*
Claims can be verified; results can be replicated.	Paths to success don't replicate.
Science	Craft
Landing on the moon	Parenting
Increasing the battery life of a cell phone	Choosing a career
The secretary problem (see chapter 7)	Deciding who to marry
Checkmate in three moves	Life

What was once destiny is now a decision. That's glorious, but it's also challenging and often disquieting. Choice offers the potential for a better life. But how do we navigate this landscape of freedom when there's no recipe or algorithm or app to tell us what to do?

One answer to the challenge of wild problems is to try to measure what you can, and do your best to quantify what you can't. That seems better than nothing, and the very process of gathering more information settles your nerves. You're making progress toward the right answer, you tell yourself. You're taking a step in the right direction.

But it can be a step in the wrong direction. If you're not careful, you're like the person under the streetlight searching for lost keys. Did you lose them here? asks a passerby who volunteers to help. No, says the seeker, but the light's better here. Using a flashlight to make the area under the streetlight even brighter might seem like a rational response, but if the keys are far from the light and deep in the shadows, you're only fooling yourself into thinking you're getting closer to finding them. By focusing on what you know about and can imagine, you're ignoring the full range of choices open to you.

When I made a similar point on Twitter, one of my

followers framed the challenge well with a question: If the important things are hard to measure, and the measurable things misleading, what kind of decision framework is left?

This book is my answer to that question. And it's what I would have told my friend struggling with his wild problem of parenthood if the walk we took that day had been a lot longer.

I can't tell you whether you should marry or have a child or go to law school. What I'll do here is help you think about how to face these problems without forgetting what's at stake. Drawing on insights from philosophers, economists, a football coach, some poets, maybe the greatest scientist of all time, and my housekeeper at Grand Teton National Park, I give you a philosophy for how to face the uncertainty that is our inevitable lot as humans.

Instead of spending more time trying to make the right decision, I show you that often there is no right decision in the way we usually think of the term. I give you advice on how to travel through life. Where you travel is up to you. The result is a set of guidelines not just for how to face decisions but for crafting a life well lived. And along the way, perhaps you'll have fewer butterflies and a little more serenity.

Let's start by looking at how one of the greatest scientists of all time dealt with his own wild problem.

2

Darwin's Dilemma

In 1838, Charles Darwin faced a wild problem. Nearing his thirtieth birthday, Darwin was trying to decide whether to marry—with the likelihood that children would be part of the package. Darwin made a list of the pluses and minuses related to the decision. And we actually have that list in his own handwriting from his journal.

Across the top of two pages he wrote "This is the Question," a reference, perhaps, to Hamlet's momentous question, the question Camus thought of as the fundamental question of philosophy—"to be or not to be." For Darwin, the question was to marry or not to marry.

Wild Problems

Marry	Not Marry
Children—(if it Please God)	No children, (no second life) no one to care for one in old age.
Constant companion, (& friend in old age) who will feel interested in one	What is the use of working without sympathy from near & dear friends—who are near & dear friends to the old, except relatives
Object to be beloved & played with—better than a dog anyhow	Freedom to go where one liked—Choice of Society & little of it. Conversation of clever men at clubs
Home, & someone to take care of house	Not forced to visit relatives, & to bend in every trifle.
Charms of music & female chit-chat.—These things are good for one's health.	To have the expense & anxiety of children—perhaps quarelling. Loss of time— cannot read in the evenings— fatness & idleness—anxiety & responsibility—less money for books etc—if many children forced to gain one's bread.
Forced to visit & receive relations but terrible loss of time	(But then it is very bad for one's health to work too much)
	Perhaps my wife won't like London; then the sentence is banishment & degradation into indolent, idle fool

On the left-hand side he tried to imagine what it would be like to be married. On the right-hand side he tried to imagine what it would be like not to marry.

Darwin was trying to imagine the daily pluses and minuses of married life and how those pluses and minuses would feel when he experienced them in the future. My friend and his wife who were struggling to make a decision about having a child had done the same thing. This would seem to be the essence of rationality. Make your best estimate of your expected well-being from one decision versus another. Choose the one with the highest expected well-being. Sure, you can't know how things will actually turn out. And surely it depends on who you end up marrying. But you do the best you can with the information you have.

Making a list of pluses and minuses seems like a good idea for dealing with any problem, wild or tame. Darwin didn't invent the technique. It's probably as old as Eve in the garden facing the wild problem of whether to eat that fruit. (Minuses—will annoy the Head Gardener, ignorance is bliss, gaining knowledge may come with unexpected downsides; Pluses—Snake seems like a pleasant fellow, forbidden fruit is sweetest, and so on.) But as we'll see, the cost-benefit list that Darwin constructed threatens to lead him badly astray. Let's take a look at his list.

The "terrible loss of time" suggests that Darwin was deeply worried about how marriage might reduce his scientific output. In his autobiography, Darwin speaks of the Baconian method—the scientific method that sprung from Francis Bacon's writing. Bacon, though not widely read today, was lord chancellor to King James I and arguably the most brilliant man of his day; he was still well-known in Darwin's England more than two centuries later. I wonder if Darwin was haunted by Bacon's essay "Of Marriage and Single Life," where Bacon argued that only the unmarried can achieve greatness.

> He that hath wife and children hath given hostages to fortune; for they are impediments to great enterprises, either of virtue or mischief. Certainly the best works, and of greatest merit for the public, have proceeded from the unmarried or childless men; which, both in affection and means have married and endowed the public.

"Hostages to fortune." Bacon was definitely onto something there. Once you are married with children, you lose a lot of control over your destiny. You are held hostage by the random, unavoidable events—what Bacon meant by "fortune"—that strike our loved ones. And of course the non-you members of your household have expectations about how you spend your time and money. You might find yourself abandoning the city you love for a more rural existence, just for starters.

Bacon, by the way, may not be the most reliable authority on married life. He didn't marry until he was forty-five, marrying Alice Barnham around the time of her fourteenth birthday; he had first noticed her as a "handsome maiden to my liking" when she was an eleven-year-old. They never had children. A few months before his death, Bacon wrote Alice out of his will for "great and just causes." Eleven days after Bacon's death, Alice married her estate's steward. You don't have to be Sherlock Holmes to connect those dots. Bacon's personal experience just might have colored his view of marriage.

But it was not unreasonable for Darwin to worry that married life—and especially married life with children—could be a drag on his scientific productivity. He rightly understood that marriage with children would reduce his autonomy. He shows no sign of being interested in children other than as a form of retirement insurance and the unavoidable collateral damage that came along with being married, describing them in his journal as a source of "expense and anxiety."

Decades before Darwin's marriage dilemma, Benjamin Franklin, who we often forget was an excellent scientist, suggested a technique for making a list like Darwin's a little more practical.

In 1772, Joseph Priestley—who would go on to discover oxygen—was considering a career change that would give him a much higher standard of living. But it would involve having a wealthy patron whose friends and society were alien to him and his wife. It might turn out very badly. He turned to his friend Benjamin Franklin for advice. Franklin wrote to Priestley, saying that while he could not tell him the right choice, he could give him a method for making the decision, a way to make his wild problem a little bit tamer.

Franklin told Priestley to take a piece of paper and draw a line down the middle, creating two columns, one of pros and one of cons. The virtue of this technique, wrote Franklin, was that when we face a wild problem, our mind will sometimes focus on one set of effects and then later on another. By taking a few days to try to accumulate all the pluses and minuses, we can survey them all at the same time.

So far, it's not much different from what Darwin did, but Franklin takes it a step further. He encourages Priestley to look at the pros and cons and "endeavour to estimate their respective Weights." When he sees a pro that is of roughly the same magnitude as a con, or three pros that add up to two cons, they cancel each other out, and he should cross them out. And by doing so Priestley can find out "where the Balance lies" and thereby "come to a Determination accordingly."

Franklin does concede that such an exercise has a large subjective component. He writes that "tho' the Weight of Reasons cannot be taken with the Precision of Algebraic Quantities," such a strategy reduces the odds of taking a "rash Step." Franklin calls his framework "Moral or Prudential Algebra," an early attempt to make decision-making mathematical and rigorous.

About two hundred years after Franklin, the Nobel laureate and psychologist Daniel Kahneman suggested doing

[handwritten margin note: Ben Franklin's approach to Pros/Con list.]

something similar when you're trying to decide on the best job candidate when you're hiring someone. If you're not careful, you might be charmed by someone's personality or by a misleading first impression. Or a gut reaction to some attribute or another could cause you to overvalue a candidate. Better to decide in advance the top six attributes that are important to the job, and assign each candidate a score from 1 to 5 on each attribute based on the interview, conversations with references, a writing sample, and whatever else you have. Then add up the scores and hire the person with the highest score.

Here's how the system would rate two candidates, Alice and Bob:

Hiring
a
candidate

Attribute	Candidate A	Candidate B
Technical skill	5	3
Reliability	5.	2
Sociability	2	3
Verbal ability	1	5
Writing ability	3	1
Work ethic	5	3
TOTAL	21	17

Bob comes across much better in the interview—he has better verbal ability and social skills. But Alice has strengths that may not come through in the interview. Using the full array of characteristics that you care about, you can get a more objective measure of which candidate is best. And if you think the six skills are of different importance, you can weight them accordingly to produce a numerical score.

Such a system takes a complex human being and boils them down to a number. In mathematical terms, this system takes a matrix—an array of numbers, a table—and converts it into a simpler thing, a single number.

When you consider buying a house, you look at its location and how many bedrooms it has, the size of the kitchen, and so on. But every house has irregularities and different shapes. So we usually rely on a single number— the square footage—to figure out which one is bigger. I may care independently about the size of the kitchen because I love to cook (or don't care about cooking at all), but the square footage sure beats a list of the different rooms and their respective sizes. The ability to boil complexity down to a single number so you can make comparisons is very powerful.

[handwritten margin notes: Boils a human to a number]

[handwritten margin notes: Buying a house]

The mathematical name for a number that describes physical concepts like area is *scalar*. Its origin is the Latin word for *ladder*, "scala"—something that helps you to climb. It's the same Latin word for *scale*—either a noun, to name things that help you measure, or a verb, as in to scale the highest peaks, to rise.

Scalars make it easy to put things on a single scale, to make them comparable. They simplify complicated things. We are really good, as humans, at heavier, higher, taller, shorter, bigger, smaller. We are really good at comparing numbers and deciding whether one is bigger, smaller, or the same as the other: 1,000 is bigger than 10; 17.3 is bigger than 17.1. Making these comparisons is so easy we do it without thinking.

Franklin's advice to Priestley is essentially the same thing. By looking for combinations of pros and cons that are roughly equal, he's implying there's a scale that allows the pros and cons to be measured in some approximate way and assessed versus each other.

A matrix is messy. Its lessons are opaque. A scalar is clean and precise. The precision makes scalars seductive. But the usefulness and accuracy of a scalar depends on how many corners have to be cut to turn a complex set of information into a single number.

On the surface, Kahneman's solution for hiring—forcing people to assign a number—makes the decision more accurate, precise, scientific. As Kahneman writes in *Thinking, Fast and Slow*, "Whenever we can replace human judgment by a formula, we should at least consider it."

Maybe I Should Read

If we are not careful, we forget those last four words and mistakenly feel that whenever we can replace judgment with a formula, we should do so. We are always searching for a formula, a calculation that will remove the uncertainty. Formulas are simple. That's a feature, but also a bug. Life is complicated.

Assigning scores to the relevant characteristics of a job candidate takes the subjective information embodied in a rambling interview and turns it into something that seems objective—a single number. This urge to quantify, to transform subjective or subtle qualitative information into something more precise, such as a single number, is hard to resist. It promises the possibility of converting a wild problem into a tame one. When it comes to decision-making, scalars—raw numbers like the index constructed for Alica and Bob—allow us to imagine we can make reliable comparisons, and that in turn encourages us to imagine it is possible to look into the future and make the best decision among the choices facing us.

But the rationality of a cost-benefit list of expected well-being from the decisions we make in the face of wild problems is actually an illusion. Let's see why.

3

In the Dark

When Darwin was trying to decide whether to marry, the information he really wanted was how his life would turn out if he decided to marry versus how it would turn out as a single man. Making a list of pluses and minuses when facing alternative universes is a way of trying to imagine what it will be like under each choice. This seems *"Expected* rational and is a version of trying to maximize what econ- *Utility"* omists call expected utility—your expected well-being in the future.

Let's organize Darwin's list so it's a little bit easier to

see. Darwin's list mixes pluses and minuses in the "Marry" column and pluses and minuses in the "Not Marry" column. It might be easier to assess the effects of the decision if it were reorganized as the pluses and minuses of choosing marriage:

Pluses of Marriage	Minuses of Marriage
Companionship	Might have to leave London
Object to be played with, a step up from a dog	Loss of autonomy
Charms of music	No clever conversation with men in clubs
Female chit-chat	Wasting time entertaining wife's relatives
Children to take care of you in old age	Wasting time visiting wife's relatives
Maybe better health, if wife keeps you from working too obsessively	Expense of children
Someone to take care of the house	Anxiety from children
	General anxiety from family responsibility
	No reading in the evening
	Might have to get a real job to support family

Reorganizing Darwin's list makes it easier to see that
Darwin has managed to come up with a lot more minuses
than pluses if he marries and that a lot of the minuses are
about lost time. Though Darwin doesn't write it down
explicitly, it's pretty clear what he considers the biggest
minus. Channeling his inner Francis Bacon, Darwin is
worried that if he gets married, he's going to have less
time for his scientific research. He's going to be a hostage
to fortune. He's going to be less productive. He might not
become a great scientist. What to do?

I imagine Darwin inviting me to his house on Great
Marlborough Street for a drink and a conversation. I'm
flattered. I hardly know him. I've only seen him across the
room in the club we both belong to. Why has he asked me
to his home? We sit at his fireplace making male chit-chat,
trying to dispel the awkwardness. He asks me how my
week has been. Fine, I answer. He wants to know what
I'm working on. I tell him I'm writing a book on decision-
making. How providential, he responds—he'd heard as
much from friends at our club. He confesses that he's
been struggling with a decision.

I smile, relaxing now that I understand why he has

invited me over. I take a sip from the glass of Laphroaig he's set at the small table next to the high-backed armchair embracing me. I stay silent. I want to give him a chance to open up. With some unease, he passes me a piece of paper. At the top I see the heading "This is the Question." I take my time, struggling with Darwin's bad handwriting and fighting the urge to say something. I stare into the fire, trying to decide how to respond.

Should I tell him about Franklin's Moral Algebra in his letter to Priestley? Franklin was good friends with Darwin's grandfather Erasmus. Darwin's father visited Franklin in Paris. Maybe Franklin's approach and the family history will appeal to him. But I worry that Franklin will lead Darwin astray. So I decide not to mention it.

Finally, it's Darwin who breaks the silence. He wants to know what I think. I look up from the fire. I sense his discomfort. And being a mere economist in the presence of a scientific giant, I hesitate. This is the man who on his voyage on HMS *Beagle* filled 770 pages in his diary, took 1,750 pages of notes, and cataloged 5,436 skins, bones, and carcasses. Who studied barnacles for eight years. Who did a twenty-nine-year experiment on earthworms for his last scientific project, *The Formation of Vegetable*

Mould through the Action of Worms, with Observations on Their Habits. While perhaps not a page-turner, I suspect it was a pretty thorough empirical study of worms and their behavior.

How do I tell Charles Darwin that he hasn't gathered enough data?

Like all of us, Darwin was in the dark about the future. And worse, like all of us facing a wild problem, Darwin was also in the dark about how much darkness surrounded him.

In her book *Transformative Experience*, L. A. Paul uses the choice to become a vampire as a metaphor for the big decisions that are the focus of this book. Before you become a vampire, you can't really imagine what it will be like. Your current experience doesn't include what it's like to subsist on blood and sleep in a coffin when the sun is shining. Sound dreary? But most, maybe all, of the vampires you meet speak quite highly of the experience. Surveys of vampires reveal a high degree of happiness.

But will it be good for *you*—the actual you and not some average experienced by others—a flesh-and-blood human being who will live the experience in real time? Ah, different question. You have no data on that one.

And the only way to get that data is to take the leap of faith (or in this case, anti-faith, maybe) into Vampire World. Once you've made the leap and find you don't care for an all-liquid, heavy-on-the-hemoglobin diet, you can't go back.

One of the weirdest parts of the decision, as Paul points out, is that once you become a vampire, what you like and what you dislike change. As a human, you might find narcissism repugnant. But vampires find narcissism refreshing and look back on their humbler non-vampire selves with disdain for their humility. Which "you" should you consider when deciding what's best for you? The current you or the you you will become?

It sounds silly, but it's not that different from a lot of wild problems we face—whether to get married or have children or join a religion or leave the religion you grew up with. Many decisions involve burning bridges, crossing into a new experience that will change you in ways you can't imagine, including what you care about and what brings you joy or sorrow, sweetness or sadness, sunshine or shade. The photographer Jessica Todd Harper describes becoming a parent in her luminous collection of family photographs in her book *The Home Stage*: "I had

Which "You" to decide with.

entered into an alternate and strange world: a world predicated by our children. I wondered what exactly I had cared about so much before I had them."

Darwin's list tells us more about Darwin than it does about marriage. His list of pluses and minuses—especially the pluses—is the list that someone would make who has never been married and has no access to the upside of the inner life of a married man. Darwin's ignorance is part of the reason his negatives about marriage (banishment! degradation! idle fool!) are so emphatic and his positives are so mild (female chit-chat).

And notice there is almost nothing in Darwin's list that suggests he'll be sharing his life with another person other than the possible demands on his time and where he might have to live. All the pluses and minuses are related to his own feelings and what he expects to experience. You might think that's reasonable—of course what happens to him is what matters.

But there's nothing in Darwin's list about devotion to another human being, or love, or the pleasures and pains of cleaving to another person, ideally, for life, till death do you part, as was the norm in the nineteenth century. Nothing about the pleasure of making someone else happy, nothing about the opportunity to soothe his spouse's sorrows. Or how her presence and devotion might affect him, other than the chit-chat. The only hint of a shared life with someone you care about and who cares about you is the line "Object to be beloved and played with—better than a dog anyhow." It's all about him, which makes sense—he's never had a partner. How would he know about the power of a shared life?

And nothing of the downside of that embrace of responsibility except respecting her desires about where to live and spending time with her relatives. Nothing about the intangible costs that a bad marriage can bring, of being trapped by the loss of autonomy. People who feel trapped in a bad marriage lose more than the ability to work whenever they want. It's not just that you want to watch movies that your spouse doesn't like or prefer the mountains to the beach when deciding on a vacation. A feeling of regret can overwhelm all that you do and experience if you have a bad marriage.

Darwin's list draws on the outer life of marriage. Like the person looking for lost keys under the glow of a streetlight, Darwin's list draws on what he might have observed as a young man in what were inevitably brief encounters with married couples in relatively formal settings. Such encounters aren't irrelevant. But the part of a marriage that is visible to an outsider is such a small part of the experience. Most married couples in the presence of others are much less likely to bicker or expose the flaws in their relationship. The bigger mystery isn't what goes on behind closed doors when couples are free to be themselves, but rather what happens behind closed eyes when married men or women reflect on how marriage alters their sense of self and how that sense of self ripples through the rest of their experience of life.

How marriage affects sense of self

Joining a married couple for a pleasant dinner may tell you something of how the couple gets along and whether they are happy. But you have little access to their inner life. This hidden inner world creates an asymmetry as we try to imagine the world we'll be living in if we are to make the leap in the dark when facing a wild problem. Like my friend and his wife trying to decide whether to have children, the future is opaque and a good chunk of that future is simply unimaginable. When you are single, marriage and becoming a parent look like a lot of restrictions with little to be gained in return.

About five years ago, I decided to attend a five-day

meditation retreat that was spent almost entirely in silence. I worried about my ability to stay silent for all five days. I worried about the stress of silence on my psyche. Would I be able to go without checking email for five days? And I had never meditated before. Would I be able to sit on the floor or on a chair, nearly motionless for forty-five minutes at a time, multiple times a day, in silence? As the date for the retreat approached, I wondered about my ability to stick with the program for the full five days.

When we arrived, we were asked not to engage with the other participants in any way during the meditation sessions. If someone was crying—and people, including myself, cried during those sessions at times—we were told not to comfort them or ask them if they were all right. At meals, we sat in silence. If you wanted the salt or pepper or water, you were not allowed to gesture to have them passed; you got up and got what you wanted. If you walked by someone in the hall, you were not to make eye contact or acknowledge them.

Sound like fun? It wasn't. But it turned out to be one of the most extraordinary experiences of my life. I've done the same retreat twice since then. I found it emotionally overwhelming. It changed the way I think about many

an
a
Silent
meditation
retreat

things but especially myself. It softened me in ways that have stayed with me long after the retreat ended.

When I tell people about the experience, a frequent reaction is "I couldn't do it. No talking for five days. I'd go crazy." I tell them that the "not talking" was the easiest part. It was in fact incredibly liberating. As the days passed, the time spent in silence became more intense, more powerful. My waking life in those five days had a texture and savor to it that is hard to put into words. But at times it was exhilarating and nothing like anything I'd experienced before.

You may be wondering how I made the leap to attend given that before deciding to go, I, too, was in the dark. My daughter, having attended similar events, thought I might enjoy it and benefit from it. Before going, I spoke to others who had attended a similar event and asked if there were any long-term effects they appreciated, and they told me yes. So partly to get closer to my daughter by experiencing something she had experienced, and partly for what I hoped would be good for me, I decided to go. But none of the people I spoke to in advance could capture for me what those five days would really be like.

I write this not to tell you that you should go on a silent

meditation retreat. I tell you this because you might think a meditation retreat is a lot like not talking for an hour, but longer. And because you've been silent for an hour while attending a lecture, say, you presume you have the ability to imagine what it's like to go on a silent retreat for five days. But it turns out there's a nonlinear effect of being silent—you cannot imagine the accumulated power of prolonged silence until you've experienced it. You also can't imagine how going through that experience might change you beyond the five days of silence. Right now, you find the thought of enduring five (or ten or thirty) days of silence as obviously irrational. But rationality is hard to define if you don't know what it's like to experience one of the choices you're facing.

Marriage, especially marriage with children, is not adequately captured by the phrase "having to share your living space with other people who will occasionally demand to spend time with you." Marriage is a lot more than just having to be around another person a lot. That's having a roommate, not a wife or a husband. And if you're sleeping with your roommate, that still doesn't capture what it's like to be married to someone for a long time.

To Darwin, looking in from the outside, marriage is

overwhelmingly about what he's going to give up. And marriage does involve restrictions. Being married does mean you can't necessarily live where you want—you may have to leave London. You can't do what you want with your time—so marriage may mean you can no longer watch the nine hours of football you've become accustomed to on Sundays in the fall and winter. Your sexual freedom is almost certainly curtailed. It's all about "can't."

Similarly, what does it mean to have children? A lot more "can't." Parenthood is when you can't go on real vacations anymore. You can't buy that new car you want because it doesn't have a back seat. Plus, you have to save for college, pay the babysitter, buy the diapers—you can't afford that car you would have wanted anyway. Parenthood means you can't go to bed until your teenager is safely home after driving back from a party.

And that's just for a man. For a woman, the list is a lot longer: things you can't eat or drink while pregnant, health complications from pregnancy, risk of death in childbirth, and in our current culture, a much tougher set of trade-offs between work and home than a man faces and what you faced before you were a mother. Who needs that?

In his book *The Rationalist's Guide to the Galaxy*, Tom Chivers tells the story of Katja Grace, who studies the impact of artificial intelligence and who at the time Chivers meets her is thinking of having a child. To understand what it's like to have a baby, Grace acquires a robot baby that cries when it is put down and wails a number of times in the middle of the night, simulating what it's like to have to go sleepless because of a needed feeding or diaper change.

Chivers describes this as a "sensible experiment" that would allow Grace to help decide whether parenting is for her or not. I can't agree. Caring for a robot baby is about as close to the downside of parenting as being quiet during a short lecture is to being quiet for five days. The writer Elizabeth Stone said it painfully well: "Making the decision to have a child—it is momentous. It is to decide forever to have your heart go walking around outside your body."

And what about the benefits of being a parent? From the outside, married people with children are fools who have made an enormous mistake. Where's the upside? Bad drawings you have to put up on the refrigerator, pretending they're a sign of prodigious potential? Hours

quote on having a baby

spent in the cold at soccer games where no one scores, all the while listening to parents yell, "Don't bunch up!"? Reading bedtime stories to short, illiterate offspring? Having an excuse to buy a minivan? The rewards seem thin for the sacrifices that children require.

And though I was joking about the minivan, sometimes the rewards aren't rewards at all. They're torments. That's one reason people get divorced. If you want a truly negative perspective on parenting, read the poem "This Be The Verse" by Philip Larkin, though you should know that Larkin never had children. But I think the appeal and experience of being single is generally understood even from the outside. It's the upside of keeping a commitment, of accepting constraints, that's harder to imagine. At least it was for Darwin.

If, like Darwin, you're wondering whether marriage or parenthood is for you, it's not a bad idea to talk with your married friends if they're willing to share something of the ups and downs. But the willingness of married people to share the experience of marriage is quite rare. First, it's intensely personal. Intimate. Second, much of the time, we who are married may have little self-awareness of how marriage changes us. It's not something we think much about unless we're writing a book on it. Third, I think many married people are uneasy being honest about the ups and downs—they may feel inadequate admitting that their marriage isn't a 24/7 lovefest of sexual and emotional bliss even to themselves, let alone to others.

And fourth, even if we're aware, even if we're willing to share, we would struggle to put those feelings into words. Not because the feelings aren't real, or because married people become inarticulate once they tie the knot, but because the emotions surrounding human relationships are inevitably complex and nuanced.

The single Darwin might think married life will ruin his career. The married Darwin might be thrilled at the satisfactions of married life in and of themselves, and those satisfactions might even make him a more productive scholar. He might even come to love chit-chat more than he can imagine.

If Darwin knew me well enough to ask me about what it's like to be a parent, I could talk until the fire in the hearth went cold and the sky began to lighten and the streetlamps went out and the sun rose, burning off the London fog. I would tell him having children connects you to your parents and lets you come closer to them in ways you never could have imagined. That it's part of the human enterprise that's unlike almost any other part of the ride. That it's a bit of immortality. That it changes you and the way you see the world.

I would tell him to imagine that there's a new play by Shakespeare that has been discovered, some say his greatest play; it dwarfs the power of anything you've seen before. It's full of raw emotion and passion and humor and farce and disappointment and courage and fear and laughter. And often the purest joy. You have a chance to see it tonight.

Would you go? Is it a comedy or a tragedy? he asks. Alas, those who have already seen the play aren't willing or able to talk much about the experience. It's too intense. And the ending's different with every performance so there's really no point in reading the reviews. Would you want to be part of that spectacle, knowing that it can fill you with light you'll never otherwise see but that it also can break your heart and leave you in tears? And by the way, if you're lucky, there's someone you love alongside you in the dark, sharing the drama, laughing and crying with you.

Not everyone can handle it. Not everyone wants to

handle it. Not everyone is given the opportunity to handle it. But if you do become a parent, no matter how the drama turns out, the experience fills your heart like nothing else. I'm a big fan, but that's me. It may not be you.

Does that help? Probably not. That's the way it is with wild problems. Does that take some of the pressure off as you think about making a life choice? Maybe. More on that later.

For now, realize that Darwin can only pretend to make a rational decision. First, he can't imagine what the actual costs and benefits are—especially the benefits—until he has experienced them. Second, he has to deal with the vampire problem. Whose weights matter, single Darwin's or married Darwin's? Marriage with children can look pretty stultifying. Yet many parents seem to be glad they've had children. Maybe they're just fooling themselves. But even if those parents are telling the truth about their own experience, Darwin can't know if his experience will be the same.

But there's a third problem with trying to imagine what it's like to be married with children before you've made the leap. There's something missing from Darwin's attempt to plumb the reality of marriage and parenthood from the perspective of a single, childless man. I've already hinted at it here, but there's surely nothing of it in Darwin's list.

To see what's missing, let's look at some other scientists and analytical thinkers who struggled with wild problems. On the surface, these people seem to prefer emotion to rationality when making important decisions. But when we look a little closer, their choices aren't irrational. They have something profound to teach us about how to live.

4

This Is Serious

By looking at how scholars and scientists look at wild problems, we can get at what is in the shadows rather than under the streetlight when it comes to big life decisions. Let's start with Persi Diaconis, a chaired professor of mathematics and statistics at Stanford University. He's a member of the National Academy of Sciences. His research is on chance, risk, and probability. He's presumably a pretty rational guy who you'd think would have a lot of tools for making a good decision in the face of a wild problem. Yet when he faced his own wild problem, he confessed to abandoning the rational approach from his own research, a story he told in a talk on decision-making.

Some years ago I was trying to decide whether or not to move to Harvard from Stanford. I had bored my friends silly with endless discussion. Finally, one of them said, "You're one of our leading decision theorists. Maybe you should make a list of the costs and benefits and try to roughly calculate your expected utility." Without thinking, I blurted out, "Come on, Sandy, this is serious."

This sounds like a joke. What could be more serious than a careful assessment of a major mid-career move weighing the expected costs and benefits of change against the status quo? Yet Diaconis admits he wasn't trying to be funny at the time. He was in emotional turmoil over his decision—his response was "blurted out." Why was it so hard for him to calculate "expected utility"—which is economics jargon for his best guess of how he would feel about the outcome of choosing one path over another?

In the same talk in which he recounted this story,

Diaconis then says something even more shocking for a scholar of decision-making. He says that you should indeed make that list of costs and benefits, but not for the purpose of assessing them rationally. Rather, he argues, make the list in order to figure out what you're "really after." And by that he means where your heart lies. Strange. What could be a better way to get at what you're "really after" than that list of costs and benefits and your assessment of them in the cool solitude of rational contemplation?

Diaconis then cites a poem, "A Psychological Tip," by *Poem to read.* Piet Hein, a mathematician who was trained as a physicist and who liked to play what he called "mental ping-pong" with a fellow Dane, the great physicist Niels Bohr. Presumably, Hein was no slouch when it came to logic, reasoning, analytical thinking, and rationality.

In the poem, Hein says that when you face a dilemma and can't decide what to do, flip a penny in the air. Not as the way to make the decision, but as the way to discover "what you're hoping," in Hein's words. While the penny is spinning, you'll sense what you want the outcome to be. In other words—follow your impulsive reaction—your

Flip a Coin!

heart, maybe, or your gut, but not your mind. Huh? What kind of advice is this coming from a mathematician and scientist?

Phoebe Ellsworth holds a chair in psychology at the University of Michigan and is a fellow of the American Academy of Arts and Sciences. She admits to a similar reaction to Diaconis's when facing the same decision that tormented him—whether to change universities. Ellsworth mentions an "Irv Janis balance sheet," which is a fancy name for a list of the costs and benefits.

"Balance sheet"

> I get half way through my Irv Janis balance sheet and say: Oh, hell, it's not coming out right! Have to find a way to get some pluses over on the other side!

So much for rationality, or at least so it seems. Ellsworth confirmed this quote for me via email, and then she added, referencing, I suspect, consciously or not, the Piet Hein idea:

> I think one of the values of those checklists is that they stimulate an emotional reaction that tells you what you really want—like tossing a coin, where you think you

don't have a preference, but when you see how the flip came out you feel disappointed, and that tells you that you really did have a preference.

But why would a rational person want to evoke an *emotional* reaction? What does Ellsworth mean by "what you really want"? Isn't what you really want the choice that will make you happiest—the choice where the benefits outweigh the costs, and not the other way around?

And this brings us back to Charles Darwin.

I imagine getting a note from Darwin the morning after our conversation saying he had slept on his dilemma and come to a decision. He wondered if I could come by again—he knew it was a bit of an imposition but he valued my counsel and he wanted my reaction.

That night, after dinner in the club, I once again made my way to Great Marlborough Street, climbing the stairs to the sitting room in Darwin's chambers, and once again I found myself in the presence of the great man. As before, we were each seated in one of those wonderful high-backed armchairs before a roaring fire, Darwin's face illuminated by the light from the flames. As before, a small crystal glass of Laphroaig was waiting for me.

After the briefest of words between us—Darwin thank-
ing me for coming by again, and my saying that it really
was a pleasure and I was happy to be of assistance—
Darwin once again passed me the piece of paper he had
shared with me the night before. At the bottom of the
column he labeled "Marry" he had added a few lines that
summarized his thinking, an almost Joycean stream of
consciousness. In my mind's eye, I could see him from
the night before after we had spoken, pacing, talking to
. himself.

Darwin
deades
to
Marry

My God, it is intolerable to think of spending one's
whole life like a neuter bee, working, working & nothing after all—No, no, won't do. Imagine living all one's
day solitarily in smoky dirty London House.—Only
picture to yourself a nice soft wife on a sofa with good
fire, & books & music perhaps—compare this vision
with the dingy reality of Grt. Marlboro' St.

And then the great scientist writes at the very bottom
of the "Marry" column:

Marry—Marry—Marry Q.E.D.

Dingy? I looked around. OK, maybe a bit. I suppose it's hard to notice the decor when you have a chance to talk to Charles Darwin. Dingy with Darwin is a pretty pleasant combination. The "Q.E.D." that Darwin had written fascinated me—quod erat demonstrandum—that which was to be demonstrated, meaning proven. I don't think Darwin had any pretensions about the scientific nature of his decision. But as a scientist, the phrase must have given him comfort. He had in some sense solved his problem—he'd made a decision.

And from all appearances, he had ignored the information at hand and made the wrong decision. Based on what he knew and had written down, how could he decide to marry? What pushed him over the edge into the "Marry" column? An idyllic vision of a "nice soft wife on a sofa"? And why, suddenly, did the prospect of having plenty of time to work seem actually unpleasant? The time demands of marriage and children had been the biggest impediment to marriage the night before. And how had the London he so worried about losing, a loss he described as "banishment & degradation" should his wife prefer the country, become instead the unattractive "smoky dirty London"?

It was hard not to wonder whether one of the greatest scientists of all time had flipped out and done something totally out of keeping with his professional life, a life where relentless conscientiousness and curiosity carried him to greatness.

Instead, he appeared to have gone with his gut and ignored the data, imperfect though it was. He had done what Phoebe Ellsworth confessed to—there were too many negatives of marriage so he mentally added some positives to make sure it "came out right." Writing "Marry" three times, as if trying to convince himself of the wisdom of his decision, looks like he is protesting too much. The only things missing were exclamation points and maybe tossing a shilling into the air to discover whether marriage was really what he wanted. And while I actually wasn't there at the time, we do have Darwin's journal preserved in the Darwin archive in the Cambridge University Library with that "Marry—Marry—Marry" and the reference to the dingy apartment. All of Darwin's words that I've shared here are there in his own handwriting.

Normal human beings have trouble making decisions, and when we do, we often will come up with reasons that are merely an after-the-fact narrative—something we tell ourselves and others to justify what we've done or plan to do. But Diaconis, Hein, and Ellsworth are not normal human beings. They are great scholars, scientists, mathematicians, and statisticians appearing to act irrationally.

But I don't think they're really saying that we should ignore reason. They're saying that we care about something else besides what we experience or feel. They're telling us there's more than our future experiences at stake when we face a wild problem.

A list of expected costs and benefits like Darwin's that people use in decision-making is usually a summary of how their choices are going to make them feel. Will I be happier or less happy as a parent or a spouse? Will I like the new job better than the old one? If I have a job offer in Austin and one in Boston, which one will be more fun, more satisfying? Will the better seafood make up for the cold weather of Boston? Will Austin's music scene outweigh the lack of fall foliage that is part of living in New England?

These are all fundamentally utilitarian considerations. The utilitarian approach comes from Jeremy Bentham. In *An Introduction to the Principles of Morals and Legislation*, published in 1789, Bentham argued that human beings care about two things—pleasure and pain. If you have to make a decision, consider each choice and see which produces the most pleasure relative to pain. Bentham uses the word "utility" to summarize the good over and above the bad that results from an action or a policy.

Utility is whatever pleases you, both physical pleasure and psychic pleasure. Bentham calls it "benefit, advantage, pleasure, good, or happiness." On the surface, this makes sense. When we are faced with a decision, we care about making the best choice. Surely in making that choice, we would want to know how that choice is going to make us feel, not just physically but emotionally as well. Bentham's approach became the backbone of how economists view what is called rational choice.

In Bentham's view and in the economist's view of the human experience, life is something like a day at a giant amusement park where you have a fixed amount of money to spend on a finite number of rides. Because your income is finite, it isn't feasible to have or do everything you desire. Rationally, you seek out the rides that you enjoy and avoid the ones you don't. You ride some more than once as long as the pleasure you get from that extra time remains higher than the pleasure you might get from riding a different ride for the first time. The economist's view of life is that your goal is to accumulate the greatest amount of satisfaction given the constraints of income and time.

In the economist's perspective, the utilitarian perspective, life is a series of feelings—joys and despairs, pains and pleasures. But what else can there be? Isn't that what makes up a life, what we experience and how we feel about those experiences?

Maybe. But I think Darwin and the other scientists and academics discussed in this chapter were uneasy facing their wild problems because they recognized that how we feel day to day or moment to moment—what I will call narrow utilitarianism—isn't the only thing we care about.

What else might there possibly be? What made these seemingly irrational scientists go with their intuition, their instincts, something beyond what reason would suggest as the right decision?

Human beings care about more than the day-to-day pleasures and pains of daily existence. We want purpose. We want meaning. We want to belong to something larger than ourselves. We aspire. We want to matter. These overarching sensations—the texture of our lives above and beyond what we call happiness or everyday pleasure—define who we are and how we see ourselves. These longings are at the heart of a life well lived.

A life well lived is something more than a pleasant life. The Greeks called the condition of a life well lived eudaemonia. That word is sometimes translated as happiness or contentment. Those words fall short of capturing eudaemonia. "Flourishing" is a better translation and the word I will use here.

There are two everyday senses of the word "flourish." One is to be successful, usually in a material, financial sense. The second, the one I am using here, describes something organic and alive. Something flourishes by becoming something beautiful and worthy of admiration. We human beings flourish by taking our circumstances and making the most of them in fulfilling our human potential.

To flourish as a human being is to live life fully. That means more than simply accumulating pleasures and avoiding pain. Flourishing includes living and acting with integrity, virtue, purpose, meaning, dignity, and autonomy—aspects of life that are not just difficult to quantify but that you might put front and center, regardless of the cost. You don't get married or have children because it's fun or worth it. Having a child is about more than just the accumulated pleasure and pain that comes your way because there is a child in your life. You have a child because it makes your entire life richer even if it makes your bank account poorer.

The choices we make in the face of wild problems produce more than just a stream of costs and benefits going forward. Those choices define who we are and give our lives meaning when they work out well. Even the challenge of facing them when they don't work out well is part of living as a human being. For wild problems, the question of flourishing looms large.

Let's summarize why a decision like Darwin's in the face of a wild problem is so difficult:

+ He can't imagine his daily life as a husband and father, particularly the upside. So he can't assess whether the expected costs outweigh the expected benefits.

+ Even if he could imagine his daily life, he faces the vampire problem—how he experiences the costs and benefits once he's married with children will change.

♦ And finally, there are aspects of being a husband and
   father that loom larger than just the everyday experiences of life, what I am calling flourishing. How
   should he take flourishing into account?

One answer that comes easily to economists is to include aspects of flourishing in Darwin's list of costs and
benefits. Doesn't rationality mean taking into account everything that matters to you—everything that produces
satisfaction and pleasure? The rational choice is then the
choice that gives you the most satisfaction overall. In the
jargon of economics, can't you just put aspects of flourishing into the utility function—a measure of the things you
care about? That turns out to be less helpful than it might
appear. Let's see why.

Def.
of
rational
Choice

5

The Pig and the Philosopher

Let's look at Darwin's list again and add in something about life as a spouse or parent beyond narrow utilitarianism—the day-to-day ups and downs that come from the decision. I'll italicize these factors related to flourishing so they're easier to see:

Pluses of Marriage	Minuses of Marriage
Companionship	Might have to leave London
Object to be played with, a step up from a dog	Loss of autonomy
Charms of music	No clever conversation with men in clubs

(continued)

Pluses of Marriage	Minuses of Marriage
Female chit-chat	Wasting time entertaining wife's relatives
A more meaningful life	
Become who I'd like to become—a husband and parent	Wasting time visiting wife's relatives
Children to take care of you in old age	*Might not become one of the greatest scientists of all time*
	Expense of children
Maybe better health, if wife keeps you from working too obsessively	Anxiety from children
	General anxiety from family responsibility
Someone to take care of the house	No reading in the evening
	Might have to get a real job to support family

Adding aspects of flourishing to a list of expected costs and benefits seems like a good idea, and Irving Janis and Leon Mann in their book *Decision Making* include self-approval and self-disapproval as things to include alongside what I'm calling narrow utilitarian considerations. But does it help?

How would you apply Benjamin Franklin's idea of crossing out things from the minus column to offset the pluses? It's almost silly. How do you think about what you'd give up to have a more meaningful life? The question itself might make you respond, "Come on, this is serious!" What pleasure or consolation would compensate for failing to become a great scientist—the person you think you're meant to become? It's more of an example of "three of these things are not like the others" than a useful strategy for making a good decision.

But why is it so hard? A beach vacation spent sunning and reading is very different from a mountain vacation of hiking. But we usually can compare them and make a choice. Why is it so hard to weigh considerations of flourishing with the day-to-day pleasures and pains that come along with our choices when we face a wild problem?

Flourishing is both quantitatively and qualitatively different from our day-to-day pleasures and pains. Quantitatively different because purpose, meaning, dignity, and our sense of self are more important to our overall well-being than enjoying a good meal or getting a flat tire—pleasures and pains whose impacts are relatively small. But the other key difference is that the pleasure of the good meal and the pain from the flat tire are both fleeting. They come, they go. The parts of our well-being related to flourishing persist and overlay our daily experiences.

Our essence is not easily compared to our day-to-day feelings of pleasure and pain. That's because who I am in my essence lies above and beyond whatever I feel today and tomorrow. Purpose, meaning, dignity, being a spouse or parent—these aspects of our lives aren't just pleasant or unpleasant. They define us and suffuse all of our days, not just this one or that one.

John Stuart Mill said, "It is better to be a human being dissatisfied than a pig satisfied; better to be Socrates dissatisfied than a fool satisfied." That's another way of saying that who you are and how you live are more important than what you experience. Dan Gilbert, the Harvard psychologist, disagrees. Gilbert is the closest thing we have in the academic world to an expert on happiness. His TED Talk on the science of happiness has more than nineteen million views. He's also delightful, thoughtful, and funny. Gilbert argues that all that matters is our happiness as we experience it or fail to experience it over our lifetime.

Gilbert imagines being "a shameless hedonist happily swimming in my Olympic size pool, feeling the cool water and the warm sunshine on my skin and my hedonic state could only be described as pleasurable. Occasionally I jump out of the pool, pause, and think about how empty my life is, and for a few minutes I feel bad. Then I get back in the pool and swim some more." So for twenty-three hours a day, you're as happy as a pig in a pool. One hour a day, you're a philosopher, reflecting on your empty, piggish life.

Gilbert argues that each perspective is self-contained. When you're the pig, swimming in the pool or enjoying a delicious meal or an exhilarating sexual encounter, you aren't thinking about the meaning of your life or your identity, your philosopher side. You're happy, oblivious to whether your life has meaning, for example, or whether swimming in the pool is ethical or consistent with your values. In that one hour of the day when your inner Mill haunts you, sure, you're uncomfortable with the nature of your life. But in those moments, because you're wearing your philosopher hat, you've lost touch with your inner pig and fail to correctly take into account the pleasure from the choices you've made in the other twenty-three hours.

[handwritten margin note: Drop the Philosopher hat]

Gilbert's conclusion is that because each perspective ignores the other—something akin to the vampire problem—each type of experience should get equal weight. Gilbert argues that whichever experience has the longest duration—the satisfaction of the pig or the dissatisfaction of the philosopher—should carry the day. All that matters is how long the satisfactions of the pig or the dissatisfactions of the philosopher last. If your time as a pig is longer than any anguish you might feel as the philosopher, you have a good life.

Most of us, other than maybe Hugh Hefner or Socrates, are a mixture of the shameless hedonist and the wondering philosopher. We enjoy the pleasure of life. We generally prefer to avoid pain. To give day-to-day pleasure its due, think of simple contentment—the prophet Micah's description of the good life—every person under their vine and fig tree, unafraid. Or the experience of marveling at your child's first step. Or the beauty of sunlight coming through the clouds and illuminating the valley below you as you crest a hill on a satisfying hike. Surely, those moments of contentment are an important part of the human experience.

But most of us want more than just those day-to-day

moments of contentment or pleasure. We want purpose and meaning. We want to behave ethically. We care about our connections to our friends and family. We have a sense of how we should behave with those close to us. And we're willing to endure some pain to have purpose and meaning and to do the right thing. Who we are, how we see our-selves, and the paths we choose to follow are central to our most important choices. Mill is saying that's how a human being should live.

Most of us don't want to swim in the pool for twenty-three hours no matter how pleasurable it may be in the moment. The hour of self-reflection that follows creates more than an hour of disappointment. These urges and parts of our inner selves are not just things that cross our mind now and then when we happen to reflect on them while toweling off poolside. They may haunt us with regret and disappointment during all of the days that lie ahead.

On any one day, I might not enjoy being married or being a parent. In fact, there might be a lot of days like that. I could even imagine that for some spouses and parents, the number of bad days outweighs the number of good days. But most of us don't decide how to live, we don't decide who we want to be by some kind of majority rule that Gilbert argues for—by looking at the preponderance of pleasure and pain summed up over a lifetime. There's something else going on alongside the daily experiences, moment to moment. A fulfilling life, a life well lived, is about more than adding up pleasure and pain and trying to make the former greater than the latter.

A life of fifty years of pure pleasure followed by twenty years of regret and shame is not the same as twenty years of suffering followed by fifty years of contentment. The fact that timing matters—whether the good times come before or after—suggests that the good life is about more than toting up costs and benefits and seeing which outweighs the other. We care about more than just the sum of day-to-day pleasures versus pains. We would gladly endure some suffering to achieve something we value deeply even if the suffering lasts longer than the joy that comes from our achievement.

Pain turns to pleasure

For most of us, being a vampire isn't just uncharted territory. It's immoral territory. Even if everyone who makes the leap to being a vampire is wildly happy and disdainful of the pitiful mortals who don't drink blood, a lot of us think that becoming a vampire is simply wrong. We don't care how happy we'd be living forever and coming out of our coffins at night. It isn't who we want to be.

The decision to become a vampire isn't really such a wild problem. It's a very tame one. I don't want to be a vampire—it's immoral. Levels of post-vampire happiness relative to pre-vampire levels don't tempt me. And even though I know that once I'm a vampire, the immorality of my vampire life won't bother me, I'd prefer to keep my all-too-human conscience and stay as I am.

Adding up the costs and benefits is the wrong way to think about how to live. Flourishing is something subtler that overarches our day-to-day pleasures and pains. The part of existence I am calling flourishing both transcends and elevates our day-to-day experience.

When you become a parent, how you see yourself and what you see as your responsibilities change. This sense of self—this sense of being a parent—transcends your daily life experiences. Who you are is now more than what you experience. But being a parent also elevates your daily life because there is this new creature who is now part of your life. Small things you never noticed seem magical. Daily life has a different texture. And it's not all peaches and cream. You have worries and pain you wouldn't otherwise have. You are irrevocably connected to another human being and nothing is quite the same after that.

Having a hobby like golfing can be relaxing. It can be an oasis of calm and take your mind off whatever else is stressful in your life. A spiritual practice—meditation or religion—can have the same effect. But the ideal of a spiritual practice is for it to transcend the time you spend meditating or in religious devotion. It should transform you in some way and change not just what you feel but who you are. And who you are, in turn, affects how you treat others and move through the world. At the same time, a spiritual practice can elevate your day-to-day experience of beauty, of sadness, of the small and large.

Becoming a vampire doesn't just affect you when you're drinking blood or sleeping in a coffin. You're a vampire 24/7. With wild problems, your choices often produce a state of being that suffuses your days in good ways and bad. Thinking you can do a cost-benefit analysis of this transformation is an illusion.

But how can it be rational to choose to do things that bring more pain than pleasure? Who with eyes open

Spiritual Practice

would willingly choose a path that promises the possibility of more suffering and heartache than joy and delight? Who volunteers for heartache and unease?

Human beings.

We like a challenge. It's why people write haiku, join the army when there's a war on, scale seemingly unscalable heights just because they're there, run marathons, volunteer for work without pay. Pain, especially when it's in service of an ideal, can be a source of meaning. That doesn't make us irrational. It often makes us admirable.

My wife went shopping at REI for gear that she needed for a five-day hiking trip she planned with her sister. The salesperson wanted to know if it was going to be a Type 1 or Type 2 experience. The difference? A Type 1 experience is nice the whole time—nothing too stressful, mostly positive. You enjoy it while you're in the middle of it and you enjoy it after. A day at the beach. A walk in the park.

A Type 2 experience is hard. There are moments of pain that have to be endured—difficult days with a lot of altitude gained over a fairly short distance, streams to be

[handwritten marginal notes: "Type 1 vs Type 2 Experiences"]

crossed without your shoes where the water runs so cold your feet go numb while you're crossing, heavy gear to be carried on the trek that hurts your back or feet.

But a Type 2 experience is one that you never forget, one that makes you stronger, and when you overcome the obstacles in the way, you feel like you've accomplished something. A Type 2 experience can teach you something about yourself. A Type 2 experience has a chance to be more than pleasant. It can be exhilarating. You might not enjoy it (much) while you're in the middle of it. But you enjoy it after it's over and in a different way than a Type 1 experience.

And sometimes we choose a Type 2 experience that isn't just a test, but a chance to experience something profound and meaningful, a chance to share something with another person that brings out the best in us and allows us to grow. Marriage and parenting are much more Type 2 than Type 1. Most of the time, we're glad to experience them even when they're not a day at the beach. Big life decisions inevitably involve a mixture of good and bad. Those decisions create an overarching feeling that suffuses what we feel at the time and afterward.

There is a parable of the teacher who gives a student a

challenge: Here is a stone. Here is a tower with one hundred stairs to the top. Your job is to bring the stone to the top of the tower. Cradling the heavy stone, the student manages to get it to the door of the tower. But the door is very narrow and the stone is too wide. No matter how the student turns the stone, it cannot fit through the door. The task you have given me is impossible, cries the student. The teacher takes a hammer and cracks the stone open so that the pieces all fit easily through the door. The stone is your heart, says the teacher. Only a broken heart can rise upward. *Heart- break*

As we get older, we understand that the pain we have endured, especially heartbreak, hasn't just made us stronger. It has made everything we experience richer and fuller. As we get older, we come to prefer bittersweet chocolate to chocolate that is merely sweet.

In a list of costs and benefits, rather than mixing flourishing alongside what I'm calling narrow utilitarianism, it's more effective to think of each separately and to consider their relative pull in how you want to live. That forces you to bring the role of flourishing into the light. Let's look at a variety of wild problems and put flourishing alongside the day-to-day costs and benefits of our choices. As we'll see, the flourishing consequences of our choices are often decisive in driving decisions. Should they be? That's up to you. Showing what's at stake in flourishing versus what we experience day to day can help you chart your own path.

6

Flourishing Matters

When I was asked in 2020 to apply for the job of president of Shalem College in Jerusalem, I wasn't interested. As a fellow at Stanford University's Hoover Institution, I worked from home on whatever interested me intellectually. I liked my house. I liked the community I lived in. My wife and I had wonderful friendships. I was well paid. Those were the positive arguments for rejecting the job as president.

Then there were the negatives of taking the job in Israel—selling our house, trying to figure out what to store and what to bring to Israel, the fear that I might not be an effective college president, distance from family, leaving close friends behind, the fact that my Hebrew is far from fluent, and that I would have to adapt to a culture that I might not find so hospitable.

On narrow utilitarian grounds, this was a no-brainer. Only a fool would take the job. A number of friends and family told me to turn it down.

But when it came to who I am and who I want to be, it was a no-brainer in the other direction. Shalem College is Israel's only liberal arts college with a core curriculum that melds classic texts from the Western canon such as Plato and Homer with classic Jewish texts. The questions that these texts raise—the fundamental question of what is a life well lived and the answers given by Athens and Jerusalem—have become increasingly of interest to me.

As a Jew, I have long cared about the great experiment that is the state of Israel. To play a role in an institution that hopes to prepare the next generation of leaders in Israel would be a privilege close to my heart. I would be deeply involved in what is sometimes called liberal education—the process that Leon Kass, Shalem's new dean of the faculty, describes as not just "learning from" but "learning with" the great texts and thinkers of the past. To do that in a land increasingly focused on computer science and engineering at a time when what I think of as education as it ought to be is increasingly under attack in the West was deeply appealing. When the job was offered to me, how could I say no? I took the job and my wife and I moved to Israel.

Was this an irrational decision? An economist might explain it by saying that the expected benefits of self-respect and satisfaction that I hope will come from the job must have outweighed the costs of moving and giving up what I already had. And there is some truth to that. There was some pain I would not endure to take the job—a drop in income that would jeopardize our family's future. Or if my wife had opposed the decision instead of embracing the adventure and the uncertainty of the move as she did, I would have turned it down. And if the benefits had been sufficiently smaller, I would have said no: running a small liberal arts college in Bulgaria (my Bulgarian is even worse than my Hebrew; Bulgaria is not the Jewish homeland) would not have been sufficiently rewarding to make me give up what I already had.

So the narrow utilitarian part of the decision wasn't irrelevant. But the flourishing part of the decision was the decisive one. I took the job because I felt like it was something I was meant to do, a calling. To turn down the opportunity would have felt like a betrayal of the deepest parts of me.

Let's look at a variety of wild problems and see how flourishing interacts with utilitarian considerations and affects the choices people make.

Marriage and Parenthood

Darwin teaches us that marrying is about more than how I'll feel when there's another person in my bed, at my kitchen table, on my sofa. Marriage is about becoming a husband or wife. That changes who I am and how I go through life. Being a spouse transcends and elevates my daily experience.

Having children isn't just about the daily ups and downs: the pleasure of the double to right-center my kid hits in the high school baseball game or the despair of my child being rejected from the college of their choice. Wearing a robot baby tells you something about the costs of being a parent. It tells you nothing about how your sense of self changes if you have a child and how that in turn affects how you experience life. It doesn't capture how being a parent can give your life meaning.

I've emphasized the flourishing aspects of marriage and children because they are harder to see than the day-to-day experience. But for many people, flourishing means not marrying and not having children.

Franz Kafka, like Darwin, made a list in his diary of the arguments for and against marriage. Kafka, a writer; Darwin, a scientist. Kafka, from Prague; Darwin, from London. Kafka, a Jew; Darwin, at the time at least, a Christian. And yet their concerns are quite similar. Here is Kafka's list; all the words are his own (taken from *The Diaries*, 1910–1923) but I have edited it some for brevity and modern spelling. My commentary is in brackets:

1. I am incapable, alone, of bearing the assault of my own life. [So marry!]

2. Everything [about marriage] immediately gives me pause. [Uh, not so fast.]

3. I must be alone a great deal. What I accomplished was only the result of being alone. [So probably don't marry.]

4. I hate everything that does not relate to literature, conversations bore me (even if they relate to literature), to visit people bores me, the sorrows and joys of my relatives bore me to my soul. Conversations take the importance, the seriousness, the truth of everything I think. [Almost certainly don't marry.]

5. The fear of connection, of passing into the other. Then I'll never be alone again. [Ditto.]

6. In the past, the person I am in the company of my sisters has been entirely different from the person I am in the company of other people. Fearless, powerful, surprising, moved as I otherwise am only when I write. If through the intermediation of my wife I could be like that in the presence of everyone! But then would it not be at the expense of my writing? Not that, not that! [A wife might help me flourish in some ways but how can I flourish without writing?]

7. Alone, I could perhaps some day really give up my job. Married, it will never be possible. [And so if I marry, I will never be the writer I might be able to be. So don't marry—don't marry—don't marry. Q.E.D.]

And he never did. Like Darwin's list, Kafka's is obsessed with what he will not be able to do—write—which in his case meant very much being alone, and unencumbered. For Kafka, and for others, flourishing means not marrying.

Where to Live

Roya Hakakian left Iran as a teenager and came to the United States. Her book *A Beginner's Guide to America* captures the dizzying disorientation that happens when you leave the place you grew up in and move to an alien culture—lots of glorious heights alongside some serious despair from time to time. But the sequence of events that transpires when someone changes countries doesn't sum up the experience. You have to consider how moving changes your sense of self, of who you are. In Roya Hakakian's case, she became an American. That change overlays the entire experience of the ups and downs.

If you ask immigrants whether they are glad they came to America, they may extol the virtues of freedom or their relief of being free of the tyranny or economic challenges they left behind. But some or much of that retrospective look will be about what it means to be an American and how that identity infuses all of the experiences that come with moving.

Where we choose to live is about more than which place has better weather, better job opportunities, better options for day trips, better local food, and so on. Where we live is about who we are and not just what we experience.

When my wife and I moved to Israel, we became Israeli citizens, what is called making aliyah. This has a few small financial advantages, relative to a work visa. But we didn't make aliyah to save some money on taxes if we buy a car. We wanted to accept a change in our identity—our sense of self. We aspired to citizenship, to become part of one of the most remarkable national experiments in history—a people returning to a land they had last lived in with sovereignty two thousand years ago.

When the people of the United Kingdom voted on Brexit—whether to leave the European Union or stay—some focused on the financial consequences of the decision: leaving would make the British people poorer; staying was forcing the United Kingdom to subsidize the rest of the

European Union. But for many who voted "leave" and for many who voted "stay," the issue that mattered most wasn't the question of the narrow utilitarian issues revolving around their standard of living.

For many, the real issue of Brexit was identity. Did the voters see themselves primarily as British or primarily as European? Particularly in England, many who voted to leave felt that their political leaders had given insufficient attention to England as their home and insufficient attention to being English as a source of meaning in their lives. Those who wanted to stay part of the European Union embraced a more cosmopolitan, international identity.

Where to Work

When Persi Diaconis said, "Come on, Sandy, this is serious," in response to the colleague who suggested that he make a list of the pluses and minuses of moving to a different university, he wasn't saying to follow your heart or to act impulsively. I think he was suggesting that more was at stake than just where he lived. He realized that the sense of self that would come from being a Harvard professor might be different from how it felt to be a Stanford professor. To someone on the outside, it's not a big deal—they're both first-rate universities. But I think it was a big deal to Persi Diaconis. It wasn't simply about whether he'd enjoy living in Cambridge more than in Palo Alto. It was anxiety about his new self-narrative—the way he would see himself, Harvard professor—relative to his old one, Stanford professor. And surely he worried about whether his new colleagues would help him continue to grow as a scholar.

Friendship

What role should friendship play in your life? How much time should you devote to making friends and building friendships? Should you reach out to the person you met at a dinner party over the weekend? If that person from the dinner party reaches out to you, should you accept their invitation for coffee or lunch or the concert? What should you sacrifice to maintain and build the friendships you already have? How should you think about these questions? Are they best addressed by a utilitarian calculus, asking how much you get financially or emotionally out of the friendship? Should you wonder if you could be doing "better" with a different set of friends?

We often use transactional words to describe friendship—should I *invest* in my relationship with so-and-so—as if a friendship were an asset that might yield sufficient return for the time spent. But an alternative is to value friendship independently of how rewarding it is, as an essential part of your being. You might desire to be a good friend even when it isn't worth it, another financial phrase that implies a utilitarian perspective. For many of us, friendship and the web of connections we establish with our friends establishes who we are. We devote time to our friends independently of how pleasant or unpleasant the experience is from day to day. I explore the issue of friendship more deeply in chapter 8.

[handwritten margin note: Friend-ship isn't transaction]

Voting

Do you vote? Why? It's not the biggest wild problem, but whether to vote shows how our sense of self and what we think is right—parts of flourishing—are in tension with our narrow utilitarian side. Economists actually argue that voting is irrational. Getting to the polling site, waiting in line to cast your vote, and returning home all take time. Those are the costs. The benefit? If there's a tie, your vote will break the tie and prove decisive. But most of the time, it's not close to a tie. Even if the election is close—an outcome decided by a few hundred votes—your vote is still meaningless with respect to the result. But you, dear reader, may vote anyway, as I do, knowing that my vote will likely add a just a single vote to a number that is already in the millions. Why bother?

When I pose this question to people, they usually answer, But what if everyone stayed home? The economist's response is that whether they stay home or not is unaffected by whether *you* stay home or vote. So rationally, you should stay home. Instead of voting, use the time to mow your lawn or read to a child, make money consulting, or volunteer at a soup kitchen. Instead of voting, the rational choice is to find the best alternative use of your time.

Tell this to a voter and they never respond, "What a great point! If my vote is essentially worthless, the rational thing to do is to do something that isn't worthless." Instead, a person who votes gets angry at the economist. Only an economist is puzzled by this anger. People vote because they think it's the right thing to do—it is part of their identity as a citizen. They vote because they don't want to see themselves as shirkers. They want to see themselves as responsible citizens who have an obligation to vote and who believe in fulfilling their obligation. They don't see themselves as suckers for voting. They see themselves as admirable. Only an economist seduced by narrow utilitarian considerations would call that irrational.

Divorce

Darwin struggled with the decision to marry; people who find themselves in bad marriages face a similar dilemma. Whether to divorce is as wild a problem as whether to marry. In modern times, divorce has become systematically easier in most countries. And there has been a strong cultural trend toward removing any stigma from divorce. If your marriage isn't satisfying, you're encouraged to leave it. As one friend who divorced told me, "I just wasn't getting enough out of the marriage."

Economists have modeled divorce as a rational decision—you divorce when your well-being from being divorced exceeds your well-being from being married.

Certainly you can look at divorce as a social scientist using this framework. It may even lead to useful predictions and help us understand certain patterns of divorce over time and across countries. But I don't think it captures anything close to what actually is happening to people struggling in bad marriages.

Despite the cultural trend toward removing the stigma from divorce, many of the people I know who are divorced do not seem to have made a simple decision based on maximizing their well-being. Marriage is part of their identity, how they see themselves. And they know divorce will be part of their identity, too, if they choose to end their marriage. They don't like the idea of being divorced as a statement about who they are. They often see themselves as the kind of person who stays loyal until death parts them from their partner.

Some people divorce on purely utilitarian grounds in hopes of finding more day-to-day happiness than they get now from their current partner. Others find themselves so oppressed by marriage that flourishing seems impossible. For those people, divorce is about more than being happier—divorce is the path to flourishing.

Becoming Religious or Moving Away from Religion

You don't convert to a religion because you think it will be more fun to go to church or eat only kosher food or pray facing Mecca five times a day. And you don't just leave a religion because you discover it's not so much fun. There are day-to-day joys to be found in both a religious life and a life free of religious constraints. But the decision to join a religion or leave one (or avoid all religion) is not just about whether we will find the resulting life as pleasant or unpleasant. For many, a religious life is about finding truth— the costs are irrelevant. The same is true of many who lose their faith—they leave their community, even when it is deeply painful to do so, because they no longer feel that their faith is true.

Belonging is a central part of the appeal of religion and politics—the feeling that you are part of something larger than yourself, something that you believe in as an obligation or that you believe will make the world a better place. This feeling of belonging to something that matters deeply can suffuse our days well beyond the day-to-day.

Seemingly Crazy Acts of Kindness

Why did some Germans and Poles hide Jews from the Nazis during the Holocaust? Most didn't of course, but why did anyone do it, given that to do so meant risking one's own life and the lives of one's entire family? Most of us don't donate one of our two kidneys to a stranger. But why does even one person do something that risky with little apparent promise of return? When I asked the documentary director Penny Lane why she donated a kidney, her answer was that it just seemed like the obviously correct decision once she understood or thought she understood the costs and benefits. The cost was the surgery she would have to undergo and the attendant risks. The benefit was giving a stranger a better and longer life. Not exactly the standard narrow utilitarian calculus. Her expectation was that if the surgery went well, she'd have one less kidney and a stranger would have years of life free from dialysis and imminent death. We'll come back to Penny Lane's experience in chapter 9. Meanwhile, do you think she made an irrational decision? Do you think her a fool or someone to admire?

Now What?

Many people put flourishing ahead of narrow utilitarian effects when they make decisions—they focus on how they see themselves, what they consider purposive or meaningful in their lives, what they think of as right or virtuous. They choose to take these aspects of their lives into account even when the day-to-day consequences of what they will experience from their choices are more pain than pleasure.

You may choose to emphasize flourishing; you may choose to ignore it. And surely, you can flourish without voting or giving away one of your kidneys. You can spend all day in the pool trying to have as much pleasure as possible and ignoring flourishing. Maybe it doesn't matter to you. But Darwin's list of the costs and benefits of marriage shows us how easy it is to ignore the parts of life that are not easily imagined. Those parts include things you might enjoy once you've made a leap. It also might include things that yield more pain than pleasure day to day but that give your life purpose and meaning.

We understand the appeal of the sunlit pool and the

poolside margarita. Those pleasures are brightly illuminated under the streetlight of your prior experience or they're experiences you can easily imagine. It's harder to remember that there might be something more meaningful in your life if you toweled off, got dressed, and spent less time at the pool. The importance of flourishing is not just harder to remember than the pleasures and pains of our daily lives. It's more than just something you'll enjoy down the road. It's harder to conceptualize before you've experienced it.

The economist and moral philosopher Adam Smith thought that flourishing, and the contentment it produces, is trickier than it looks. In his little-known masterpiece *The Theory of Moral Sentiments*, he wrote that "man naturally desires, not only to be loved, but to be lovely." By "loved," he meant not just cared about but praised, appreciated, admired, and respected. We want to matter. And by "lovely," Smith meant worthy of praise, appreciation, admiration, and respect. And writing in 1759, when he said "man," he meant human beings. Smith's idea of being loved and lovely is very close to what I am calling flourishing here.

Smith observed there are two ways to matter—two

ways to earn the praise, appreciation, admiration, and re-spect of the people around you. One way is to be rich, powerful, and famous. The other is to be wise and virtu-ous. Smith calls the first path "gaudy and glittering." This path is naturally alluring—the rich, powerful, and famous are easily noticed and those who notice are numerous, what Smith calls the "great mob of mankind." We some-times say that a rich, powerful, famous person is flourish-ing, but it's a different sense than the one I'm using here and it leads to a different kind of satisfaction.

The path of wisdom and virtue will also earn the re-spect of those around you, but that path is not so well illuminated. It attracts the attentions of what Smith de-scribes as a "small party," mainly those who themselves are wise and virtuous. The glittering, brighter path is the seductive one. The better path is in the shadows and harder to remember.

If you care about flourishing, you have to work hard to keep it front and center.

In the next few chapters, I expand upon this idea by looking at a series of wild problems in more depth and exploring the seductiveness of what is in the light versus what is in the shadows. I suggest some approaches that might be more helpful than trying to make a narrow utilitarian calculation. There's no simple set of rules to follow for facing these wild problems. Instead, I wrestle with some common wild problems to help you discover your own approach to facing them.

Let's begin with the problem of who to marry. How should we approach this decision if we want to keep flourishing in mind and whatever else might be in the shadows? Along the way we'll learn some lessons that apply to other wild problems as well.

7

Penelope's Problem

Penelope was the wife of Odysseus, the great king and warrior of ancient Greece, whom you may also know by his Roman name, Ulysses. Odysseus goes off to the Trojan War and after twenty years, he still hasn't come home to Ithaka. Assuming that he's dead, a bunch of men come to Odysseus's house in search of Penelope's hand. A big bunch of suitors. The exact number is a little unclear, but according to one count, there are 108 of them. The suitors move into Odysseus's house. (It's a large house. More like a palace—there's plenty of room for suitors.) The suitors eat, drink, and party, feasting on Odysseus's flocks of sheep and herds of cattle, waiting for Penelope to make a decision on which of them would make the best husband.

While it's always nice to be wanted, Penelope is essentially besieged. But she seems disinterested in freeing herself by choosing one of the 108. Is she simply loyal to Odysseus? Is she hoping that Odysseus is still alive and will someday return home? Or maybe she just can't face the decision of who would make the best husband. She stalls for time.

She tells the suitors that she'll pick one when she's done weaving a burial shroud for her father-in-law. Who is still alive. This may seem a bit macabre, but in Penelope's time, you couldn't run over to Macy's and pick up a nice shroud when you needed one, or head to Brooks Brothers if you wanted something a little classier. Weaving a shroud took a long time—just creating the yarn or thread was an enormous project, and you had other fabric demands on your time—making sure the family was clothed and had plenty of blankets. You wouldn't wait for your father-in-law to die. You'd make the shroud in advance.

At night, Penelope unravels what she knits during the day. The shroud ruse works for three years (!), suggesting that the suitors don't know much about weaving (very probable), are really drunk most of the time (almost certain), or have really low expectations about Penelope's weaving ability (possible). Eventually the suitors discover Penelope's trick—one of her servants rats her out to a suitor the servant is sleeping with. The suitors redouble their pressure on Penelope to make a decision and choose one of them. Presumably not the guy sleeping with her servant.

Let's suppose that Penelope really is done with dithering and wants to find the best possible husband among the suitors. How should she decide? Let's allow her to spend time with each of the 108, one at a time. She can interview that suitor, go out for coffee, share a candlelit dinner in downtown Ithaka. Then she makes a decision on that suitor—marry or not marry. But once she rejects a suitor, she can't go back. He's lost to her. Given these rules, is there a rational strategy for Penelope to follow?

You may or may not be looking for a life partner. But there are aspects to Penelope's problem that run through all of our biggest decisions—we have multiple options. Which one is the best one? Which one is the best one if I want to flourish?

A version of Penelope's problem was posed in 1960 by

columnist and science writer Martin Gardner in *Scientific American* in a different context—it came to be known as the secretary problem. Here is how Gardner structured it. What rule should you follow when you have a number of job applicants for a position and you can interview each one and either hire or reject them? Once rejected, they move on to other options and they are unavailable for hiring.

If Penelope faces these same assumptions, there is an algorithm for her to follow if she wants to maximize her chance of marrying the best man among the 108 suitors. Interview 37 percent of the suitors—in this case, that amounts to forty interviews. Penelope won't marry any of these forty. These interviews are a way to learn about the quality of what Ithaka has to offer in the way of husbands. Note the best one of the forty. Suppose the best of the first forty turns out to be Elatus. You don't marry Elatus—after all, you've turned him down so he's lost to you. But you use Elatus as a measuring stick—the benchmark—for the remaining sixty-eight. As soon as you reach someone better than Elatus, you marry him.

There's a chance that Elatus is the best candidate. Then none of the sixty-eight remaining candidates surpasses him. You're then stuck with the 108th suitor. In that case,

Penelope doesn't get the best husband. Assuming that she meets suitors in random order, the expected quality of the last man to be interviewed would be the average quality of the group. But of course, in actuality, the 108th man could be quite horrific. Expected well-being ex ante and actual well-being ex post can be very different.

What's impressive is that this strategy has a surprisingly high chance of giving Penelope the best among the bunch. How high? If she follows this strategy, her odds of getting the best husband are 37 percent. Not bad.

Both the proportion of the suitors you interview and the odds you'll find the best match by following this role have 37 percent in them. This is not a coincidence. In the general case, you take the number of suitors and divide that number by e, Euler's number. Euler's number can be represented in a number of ways, including the infinite series

$$e = \sum_{n=0}^{\infty} \frac{1}{n!} = 1 + \frac{1}{1} + \frac{1}{1 \cdot 2} + \frac{1}{1 \cdot 2 \cdot 3} + \cdots$$

which adds up to roughly 2.71828 . . . where the ellipsis represents an infinite number of digits after the decimal point. If you interview n/e suitors (where n is the number of suitors—in Penelope's case, 108) and pick the first one who exceeds your benchmark, your Elatus, the odds of getting the best candidate among the *n* suitors is 1/*e*, which comes to 37 percent. Why *e* should figure into this calculation is one of those elegant mysteries of mathematics. How beautiful is that?

Penelope did not subscribe to *Scientific American*. So she had no equation or elegant strategy for choosing among the 108 suitors. She did not rely on intuition, at least on the surface. What to do?

Of course, the reader of the *Odyssey* knows something Penelope doesn't, which is what makes her problem so riveting to the reader: Odysseus is alive and safely back in Ithaka. After surviving the Trojan War and overcoming the Sirens, the Cyclops, Scylla and Charybdis, and other challenges, Odysseus manages to make it home only to discover he has 108 enemies living large in his living room and depleting his estate. Subterfuge is going to be necessary to reclaim his wife. He disguises himself as an old beggar.

Perhaps sensing that this beggar is her husband or just continuing to stall for time, Penelope devises a test of strength as the way to solve the wild problem she faces.

First, she tells the suitors, you have to string the bow of Odysseus. Then you have to shoot an arrow through the gaps in twelve axe handles. Pull off this double dare, she says, and I'm yours.

Alas for the suitors, not one is strong enough even to string the bow. Penelope appears to be destined for a lifetime of loneliness. But the old beggar who we know is Odysseus asks for a chance, a request that is met with a chorus of anger and mockery from the suitors. How is this bent-over shell of a man going to string the bow of the great Odysseus, a bow that none of them are able to string? But Penelope suggests that hospitality demands that the beggar be given his chance. And with that announcement, she goes off to bed and cries herself to sleep, weeping for her long-lost husband, presumably unaware that he is downstairs in the flesh.

The suitors jeer and taunt this tramp in rags for thinking he can possibly pull off such a feat. But stringing the bow for Odysseus is no harder than it is for Mark Knopfler to replace a broken string on his guitar. And then, maybe just for show, Odysseus completes his wife's challenge and pulls off the arrow-and-axe-handle feat, too. The suitors know they're in big trouble. Odysseus, his son

Telemachus, and two trusted servants then proceed to kill all 108 suitors with minimal damage to themselves. And a genre is born—the small plucky band of good guys overcomes great odds and survives unharmed.

Penelope's seemingly silly test to string the bow did actually manage to identify something close to the best man. She got just a little lucky. Ending up with the best isn't something you see every day. I wouldn't count on it.

What can we learn from Penelope?

Even without the mathematical knowledge of a Leonhard Euler, and even without having a transcendental number named after your first initial, it's a good idea to get some information about prospective partners and to use that information to help you decide who to marry. You don't have to read *Scientific American* to realize that no matter how many fish are in the sea, you can't meet all of them, so consider having an implicit if not explicit stopping rule—a rough idea of when to get serious about deciding to marry.

Most of us also realize that not everyone we want to marry wants to marry us. Most of us also realize that saying no to someone risks the possibility that they will not be available down the road. I have a friend who took long overnight canoe trips with his family when his children were young. When it came time to figure out where to stop for the night, he let his children make the decision. He wanted them to learn that the best can be the enemy of the OK: waiting for the best island to camp on for the night risks getting stuck sleeping on a rocky shore or not sleeping at all. Wait for the best marriage partner and you might get stuck with the last suitor—or suitor 109 and counting.

But the most valuable lesson from Penelope's problem and the mathematical solution purporting to solve it is more of an anti-lesson. The mathematical version of the question of who to marry is elegant but not so good for living. With wild problems, the quest for the best is a mistake, whether it's the quest for the best career, the best place to go to college, the best spouse, the best anything.

For some problems we face, the best is fairly well defined. When Dan Gilbert's shameless hedonist is trying to get the most pleasure from making choices as a consumer— which shoes to buy, which hotel to stay in, which movie to watch tonight, which tequila to put in that poolside margarita—there are so many tools to help: recommendations from Amazon, reviews on IMDb, Tripadvisor, and *Wirecutter*. There's no absolute best, but usually I can get close to what's best for me when it comes to shoes, hotels, movies, tequilas, and the narrowest utilitarian areas of life.

But what is the best spouse? By best, I mean not the best one in the world but the best one who is available to me and who is a willing partner. The mathematical version of Penelope's problem assumes away the hardest part of the problem. It assumes that after interviewing forty suitors, Penelope can identify the "best" of the first forty, Elatus in my retelling. But what does that even mean? How can she possibly know who of the first forty she interviews will make the best husband?

If you give me two flavors of ice cream, I can usually tell you the one I prefer. Give me a choice between two different vacations—the beach versus the mountains, say— and I can tell you which I'd rather experience. Give me two potential spouses and let me spend some time with each and I might be able to tell you which one suits me better. But it's more of a wild guess about a wild problem than any kind of sure thing. There's not much science there.

Human beings are imperfect, flawed, difficult to live

with, sometimes even difficult to tolerate. There is surely someone smarter than your current partner, kinder than your current partner, more physically attractive than your current partner, funnier than your current partner, more patient with your faults than your current partner—the list goes on and on.

But there are very few people, maybe none, who are all of those things. How do I choose between one suitor who is sweeter than my current best romantic friend but less intelligent? Or one who shares more of my interests but with whom I have less chemistry? What are the weights I should use to trade off one attribute I care about against another?

The word "best" implies a scalar—a unidimensional measurement—a number that I can use to compare two choices. That's not the worst thing to do when it comes to hiring a job candidate, as Kahneman suggests. But choosing a life partner is a little more complicated. A life partner is the ultimate matrix of characteristics, virtues, vices, pluses, minuses. A human being. And how you experience that matrix changes over time as you ideally grow alongside your spouse. In marriage, there's more than one goal you care about.

So not only do you not know the best number of suitors to consider (though we would probably all agree that it is probably less than 108), there's no obvious way to define the best either as a benchmark or as an outcome.

A common response to this argument is, "Yeah, yeah, yeah, of course I can't find the best person. But the goal is to get as close as possible, right?" The same issue arises in many areas—better to quantify it as much as you can, goes the argument, even if it's not perfect. But this argument assumes that you will not be seduced by the precision of the measurement, even though you are aware of its imperfection. So, yes, the perfect is the enemy of the good. But the almost perfect can be just as dangerous.

You might respond by saying that it's wrong to "settle," to be content with someone who is merely OK rather than someone great. Actually, I'm saying something worse. I'm not encouraging you to settle; I'm telling you that you have to settle. The best spouse/partner/career/city doesn't exist and it's not just because they're hard to find. It's not a meaningful concept.

This is the insight of social scientist Herbert Simon, who argued that optimization (finding the best outcome) is beyond our human limitations. What I'm calling "settling" here is closely related to what Simon called "satis-ficing," a combination of satisfying and sufficing, doing the best we can with our limited knowledge. In formal models, satisficing involves a minimum threshold—at least as good as Elatus, say—to avoid the fruitless search for the best. But in general, satisficing is indeed the best we can hope for even if all we care about is narrow utilitarian factors.

The fear that we're settling can paralyze us—it can be an excuse to not make any decision at all. "Settling" isn't the right word anyway. Settling means to willingly accept an inferior option. When it comes to marriage or all kinds of wild problems, inferior is rarely on the table. We face options where some aspects of the decision appear better than others but other aspects are worse. What some people call "settling" is simply realizing that it is time to make a decision and there is no reason to think there is a better option. That's not settling. That's de-ciding.

Marriage is a case where the best is truly the enemy of the good enough. Why is marriage so hard? We don't move from city to city because we're not sure we've found the best possible city to live in. But we do sometimes struggle to settle down with a partner because of fear that we could do better. Or a bigger problem—our fear that the person we're marrying isn't the person we've always seen ourselves marrying, someone of the perceived quality to match our own perceived quality, whatever that means.

Who to marry might be one wild problem where an app or an algorithm might be helpful. Sites like Match and eHarmony try to find people who are compatible with each other. I was on the advisory board of eHarmony for a brief time. An insider there recently spoke to me about the question of finding a good marriage partner.

His view was that the power of eHarmony's algorithm that purported to find you a good or even the best match available using responses to its questionnaire was not the key to its success. It was much simpler than that. The success was due to matching people who were serious about getting married. Both the considerable length of the required questionnaire and the questions on it select for people who are serious about marriage rather than just dating. That's a useful insight for anyone looking to marry. If you're eager to get married, try to date people who are serious about marriage.

The question of who to marry illustrates the full complexity of a wild problem. You can't anticipate what the day-to-day existence with another person is going to be like. Even if you could anticipate the day-to-day existence, you can't anticipate the flourishing part of the decision—whether you're going to like who you'll become as a spouse and especially as a spouse of this particular partner.

So what do you do now? In modern times, we typically look for love and try to imagine who we'll be the most happy with. But what about flourishing? How can keeping flourishing in mind help you choose a life partner?

Here's a way to think about this kind of wild problem; it may help you beyond choosing a spouse.

Suppose you have a chance to spend three weeks in Rome, and you believe it will be your only chance to see the city. You know that Rome is home to extraordinary museums, marvelous outdoor sculptures, and ruins from ancient times somehow still standing. There is divine food to eat, luscious wine to drink, narrow streets to explore.

Beyond the standard tourist highlights, you would like to spend time just walking without an explicit destination in mind, being what is called a flaneur, wandering not aimlessly, but thoughtfully, appreciating the morning light on the walls of the ruins of the Colosseum, standing on a bridge spanning the Tiber as a rower passes below you, watching the sunset from the Spanish Steps, just taking Rome in and being grateful for the chance to see it.

Of course you want to have a good time, but you also hope to grow from the trip, learn something about the history of the city that goes back more than two thousand years, and maybe have a spiritual experience along the way. And while you are not an opera fan, you wonder if you might learn to appreciate it before your trip to the country of Verdi and Puccini.

As you prepare for your trip, you discover to your disappointment that the people you know who have been to Rome struggle to put into words what they found special about the city. They are uneasy making any specific recommendations. When you enter "Rome" into Google, it only pulls up Rome, New York. Amazon has no guidebooks for the city, and the only one you can find in your local library is from the 1940s and all the pictures are in black and white. What do you do now? You pride yourself on your rationality, but how do you make a rational decision about what to do in Rome when you're mostly in the dark about what there is to do in the city and whether you will enjoy it or not?

Life is a lot like trying to plan a trip to Rome without a guidebook.

Even if all you care about is having a good time during your all-too-short time on this earth, you will struggle to anticipate what it is that will bring delight, pleasure, contentment. And most of us care about more than just having a good time. We would like to find purpose and meaning. We would like to do the right thing. We would like to belong. We want a life well lived. We want to flourish.

You can't anticipate what you're going to enjoy, and you certainly can't imagine some of the deeper pleasures that define us beyond the narrow day-to-day experiences of life.

Start by facing your ignorance. Wild problems are not the kinds of problems with answers. And that's OK. It's better than OK. It's glorious, something like going to Rome for the first and only time. Sure, some of us would love for someone to give us an itinerary to go with our trip to Rome—a tour bus where all the stops are preplanned because they're the popular ones. But most of us would prefer to discover for ourselves what we love about Rome and what we might come to love. Wouldn't you rather be surprised than have it all mapped out for you? And it doesn't matter, because you can't map it out anyway.

But what do you do when you get to Rome without a guidebook?

One thing you might think about is traveling with someone who can help you discover what Rome has to offer. Someone to talk with after you've been to the Colosseum. Someone whose joy at seeing Michelangelo's *David* on your day trip to Florence mirrors your joy and makes it even greater.

Who might make a good traveling companion? Someone whose company you enjoy. Someone who shares your tastes in food, museums, and opera. And if you like the idea of seeing if you could learn to love opera, someone curious as well. If you hate museums, you might not want to travel with an art lover who wants to spend two days at the Vatican.

No guidebook, not even the best one, can tell you who to travel with. If you can, marry your best friend, someone you can talk to and someone you can stay quiet with. Someone who has a good heart and shares your view of

what's important—your values and principles. Find someone you respect and who respects you. Find someone who
makes your heart sing—call it love or chemistry. That's
not just good enough. It's fantastic. It's not a quest for the
best mate but the person you can explore life with at your
side, the person to share the journey with. And maybe
you can find a person who respects your imperfections
and at the same time helps you to aspire to be someone
better than you are now.

It's also not a bad idea to keep tradition in mind. I
think most of us in modern times disdain tradition as the
equivalent of superstition. It's not a bad idea to think of it
instead as what has survived the test of time. Not everything that survives is necessarily worthwhile. You might
not bow to tradition, but it's not a bad starting place.

Tradition
≠
Superstition

In this case, marrying someone who is like you, who
comes from a similar background, who shares a religion
or lack of one, who has a sense of humor, and so on, is not
advice to be dismissed immediately as old-fashioned. Sometimes old-fashioned beats cutting-edge.

This is the idea of Chesterton's Fence, named for an
insight of G. K. Chesterton's. When you come across
something that doesn't make sense to you—a fence in the

middle of nowhere with no apparent purpose—you might be tempted to tear it down. Before you do, you should try to find out why it's there—it may have a cause or purpose that isn't obvious. That is also true of many wild problems. Marriage and children may not be for you. Marrying someone who shares many of your values or comes from a similar background may not make sense to you. But it has been the way of the world for a long time. You might not want to tear down that fence without giving it some thought. There may be a reason for the practice that you cannot appreciate.

Darwin certainly took the traditional route. He not only married despite his cost-benefit list, but he also didn't spend a lot of time trying to find the best wife. And he married someone very much from his own world and experiences.

After Darwin wrote "Marry—Marry—Marry Q.E.D." in his journal, he didn't go through 108 options. Different times, the nineteenth century. Within about a year of his internal dialogue about marriage, Darwin wed his first cousin Emma Wedgwood. That's definitely staying local. They were married for more than forty years until Dar-

win's death in 1882. They had ten children; seven survived to adulthood.

How did marriage turn out for Darwin?

Twenty years after he married, Darwin published *On
the Origin of Species.* Thirty-two years into his married life,
he published *The Descent of Man.* Along the way he published books on orchids, vegetable mold, and insectivo-
rous plants. And a biography of his grandfather Erasmus
Darwin. And an autobiography. It's a shame—had he
never married, he might have made something of himself.

That joke masks the reality that there is no right decision. Darwin could have married a woman who made
him miserable; his marriage could have cost him the serenity needed to do great science, and the social norms of
the day might have prevented him from divorcing. He did
recount in letters to friends how he was unable to work
when his children were ill and that he feared he had
passed on some forms of chronic infirmity to them. A few
of his children died young and caused him great pain.

The burdens of marriage and fatherhood could have
ended up costing Darwin his place in history; Alfred
Russel Wallace could have been a lot more famous. It

[margin handwritten note: Darwin during Marriage]

seems to have turned out well for Darwin, although late in his marriage, his scientific views and his wife's religious views made their relationship more complicated than in their earlier days together.

Unlike Bacon, Darwin seems to have found a good partner and one who helped him flourish in unexpected ways. In his autobiography, after talking about his wife's kindnesses, he concluded:

> I marvel at my good fortune that she, so infinitely my superior in every single moral quality, consented to be my wife. She has been my wise adviser and cheerful comforter throughout life, which without her would have been during a very long period a miserable one from ill-health. She has earned the love and admiration of every soul near her.

He did end up leaving London. He came to enjoy the countryside. More than chit-chat on the sofa, his daily routine included a number of times each day when Emma Darwin read out loud to her husband. Evidently, he enjoyed that, too.

But I suspect his marriage to Emma meant a lot more

than a pleasurable set of life experiences. In a letter to Emma Wedgwood the week before he married her in January 1839, he made it clear that he not only aspired to be married but he aspired to be a better man than he was when he was single. Darwin saw his wife-to-be as the companion who would accompany him on his journey through life and in doing so make his life more meaningful, even more meaningful than his pursuit of scientific truth, by the opportunity to have someone at his side. He has already come to the view, perhaps through maturity or courtship, that his list of costs and benefits of marriage was incomplete.

Darwin begins his letter by hoping that through marriage he "shall gradually grow less of a brute." He goes on to say, "I think you will humanize me, & soon teach me there is greater happiness, than building theories, & accumulating facts in silence & solitude. My own dearest Emma, I earnestly pray, you may never regret the great, & I will add very good, deed, you are to perform on *the* Tuesday: my own dear future wife, God bless you."

Darwin surely didn't find the best wife. That's a fool's errand. But he did find a partner who helped him flourish.

There's one more issue with applying Martin Gardner's

Scientific American problem to your personal life. It presumes that anyone you ask to marry will be happy to have you. In real life, few of us enjoy that luxury. Penelope had 108 suitors. Many of us are lucky to have just one and sometimes that one is not necessarily a good fit.

Because it takes two to tango, many people never marry. They never find a good match. This is particularly true in modern times where the tradition of marrying young died decades ago. Friendship, rather than marriage, is another way to flourish. Many of my unmarried friends create extraordinary friendships; because they have no spouse or children, they have more time to spend on friendship, and they devote themselves to being good friends, good uncles, and good aunts. Their friendships become a bigger source of meaning and flourishing than friendships outside of marriage do for many married couples.

Most people would agree that friendship and family are deep sources of meaning. But how we interact with our friends and family is a special kind of wild problem. It doesn't have the drama of marriage or parenthood, but how we use our time and the consequences of our choices are often hard to anticipate. It's a big challenge not because it's dramatic but because much is at stake. "What's in it for me" looms large in how we spend our time—it's so easy to tell ourselves that we can spend time with family and friends later. They are there for us after all—they're our friends and family.

Our work and desire for success at work pull us away from those relationships. When it comes to family, we can rationalize spending more time at work because we tell ourselves that we're not doing it for ourselves, we're doing it for them—my family will be the beneficiaries of that promotion I'm working toward or of the higher salary my time at work will eventually produce.

We can rationalize spending time at play away from our family, too, whether it's golf or watching football or spending time fiddling on our phones. We need that play, we tell ourselves, as a form of relaxation so that we can be better friends or better spouses or better parents. Those pleasures easily seduce us—they're always in the glare of the streetlight. It's natural to see ourselves as the center of the universe. How can we remember the importance of friendship and family?

Every day, we face the question of how to interact with those around us. What kind of friend or parent or colleague do we want to be? This question doesn't have the drama of proposing marriage or giving birth to a child. But how we act as friends, parents, colleagues—how we treat those around us—defines us even if that definition unfolds almost imperceptibly over a long period of time compared to the more dramatic life decisions. Every day, we can see those around us as a way to flourish or as a way to achieve a more utilitarian pleasure. Often these two forces compete. In the next chapter I explore how you might think about that competition to become who you'd like to be.

8

How to Get Over Yourself

There's a saying of unknown origin: If you want to go fast, go alone. If you want to go far, go together. I have never minded going alone. Both my wife and I have what the poet Dana Gioia calls "a capacity for solitude." And it's a capacity worth cultivating in today's world of attention-grabbing apps and screens. But for longer journeys, my wife and I both prefer each other's company. The principle extends well beyond marriage—so much of what we do as workers, as volunteers, as joyful players of the games that delight us, we do with others. Cooperation is under-appreciated.

Playing well with others—being a good friend or spouse or colleague—is a wild problem we confront every day, trying to balance our work or our desire to be by ourselves with the desires of the people around us to spend time together. How does a focus on flourishing help us deal with this tension? How can we be better friends, better spouses, better colleagues?

Getting over yourself is a good place to start—being aware that you're not the center of the universe. That requires some level of self-awareness—being aware of how your actions and words affect others and how you're perceived. Self-awareness can come from therapy, meditation, religion, or reading philosophy or literature.

Religion and meditation at their best put us in touch with not just ourselves but what is larger than ourselves; they let us experience the transcendent as well as a feeling of belonging. At their worst, these practices can devolve into a form of self-absorption and narcissism, a form of navel-gazing and self-centeredness. I'm talking about something different here. I'm talking about being aware that what we say and think is often subconscious. Our buttons get pushed by what happened earlier in the day or by a habitual form of interaction with others that be-comes a rut that is hard to escape.

In a marriage, for example, one partner might react viscerally to something said by the other, a reaction that has been honed over time to be totally subconscious. At its best, what meditation or therapy or religion can do is to allow a pause before the response. That pause can help you realize that what is really going on is not always cap-tured by the words. The pause can remind you that you can step out of the script that you might otherwise be stuck in. The pause can remind you that your natural re-sponse is mediated by your own fears, desires, and needs. The pause can remind you that you can step out of your habitual response and be more considerate or thoughtful. With practice, you can change your habitual response to a better one.

One of the challenges of cultivating this kind of self-awareness is that it doesn't seem to come naturally. And the narrow utilitarian approach to life makes self-awareness harder. If I'm always asking, What's in it for me?—What benefit will I enjoy, and is it greater than the cost?—it's harder to notice how I interact with others and how the way I'm behaving may not be considerate of what they might need from me.

How can we break free of the scripts we repeat over and over as if on autopilot, the scripts that deaden or poison our relationships? How might we rewrite our personal narrative, what we might call the story of our life, in a way that can help us get over ourselves? We get used to the narratives we have of ourselves—victim, hero, superstar, loser, and everything in between.

Inevitably, we see ourselves as the main character of our own reality show. As the main character, you face those big life decisions—where to live, what job to take, who to marry, and so on—the wild problems of your life. Along the way, as in any good drama, life intervenes in all kinds of typical and unexpected ways, the plot twists that make a story interesting. You get sick; a job offer you're expecting doesn't come through; a romantic opportunity ends in rejection. Or you receive an unexpected honor; a friend starts a business and makes you an offer you never expected; that trip with a friend turns into love.

Through all of this, you persevere and give up, smile and cry, dance and sit on the sidelines, plan and plot, hope and dream. You daydream about the successes of the past and the ones you can imagine in the future. You congratulate yourself on the plot twists that turned out well, and often, but not always, you remember darker episodes or even a whole season of not-so-cheerful episodes, where things hadn't gone so well despite your best efforts. The past is an ever-increasing archive of stories—the memories you take with you into the future—and the future holds all the stories you hope to craft.

Because we're hardwired to think about ourselves more than we think about others, we have this internal drama called "the story of my life" going 24/7 on our inner video screens. So it's normal to think of yourself as the main character of the drama that is your life and everyone else around you as the supporting cast.

This narrative fills our headspace and in turn affects how we experience our day-to-day lives. It is the way we make sense of what happens to us and what we hope will happen in the future. These narratives are inevitably incomplete. As the scriptwriters, we tend to fashion our inner narratives in ways that focus on ourselves, and in ways that are not necessarily accurate.

Adam Smith was aware that how we see ourselves doesn't always correspond to how we really are.

He is a bold surgeon, they say, whose hand does not tremble when he performs an operation upon his own person; and he is often equally bold who does not hesitate to pull off the mysterious veil of self-delusion, which covers from his view the deformities of his own conduct.

As the authors of our own narratives, we often struggle to see the truth about the main character. The "mysterious veil of self-delusion" is hard to lift.

In the old days people presumably saw themselves as the authors of their own novels. We moderns are more cinematic. So from my perspective, my life story is something like *The Truman Show* with me in the role of Truman. With a lot fewer viewers. Well, actually, just one viewer. Me. I'm the main character and I'm pretty much the only one who sees the story that way, but most of the time I never notice. I'm too busy thinking about the script and the episodes that have come before and those that are still to come if the series gets renewed.

There's a different way to think about our lives. Not the storytelling part, which is pretty much hard-wired alongside the self-centered part, but the main character part. Inevitably, if you see yourself as the main character of your own reality show and people around you as part of the supporting cast, you miss a big part of life and who you can be as you experience it.

Our natural impulse to see ourselves as the main character inevitably assigns less important roles to those around us. Imagine a middle-school production of *My Fair Lady*. The director of the musical went to high school with Benedict Cumberbatch and somehow convinces him to play Eliza Doolittle's father, Alfred, the dustman.

Alfred isn't the star of the musical. But he does get two great songs—"With a Little Bit of Luck" and "Get Me to the Church on Time"—and some wonderful dialogue. Put Benedict Cumberbatch in that role with a bunch of middle-school students and it would be unforgettable for most of the students. And Benedict would get some good stories out of it for his own script: "Let me tell you about the time I did this favor for an old friend of mine from Harrow . . ."

How would you describe the relationship between

Benedict Cumberbatch and a bunch of kids inevitably overwhelmed and in awe of having a real actor and celebrity in the show? Distant, is the simple answer. They're just not comparable. And because they're not comparable, they can't really have a relationship. They relate to one another in some dimension, of course. They're in the same show, after all, and share scenes together. And there's even some conversation offstage. But they don't really interact in a meaningful way. There's just too big a gulf between the star and the rest of the cast. Can Cumberbatch really share anything of his essential self when he's onstage or even offstage? That's hard to imagine. How authentic can he really be among a bunch of middle-schoolers?

I think to some extent this is the reductio ad absurdum of what we do when we cast ourselves as the main character in the story of our lives. We relate to other people, but not on an exactly equal footing. If I'm not careful, it's about how I feel more than about what you feel. If I'm not careful, it's about how your actions affect me and not the other way around. And even when my role is just someone in the chorus, I inevitably make it seem bigger than it really is. I inevitably take myself a little too seriously. I inevitably underestimate your role and find it hard to remember that you, too, have emotions and drama in your own life apart from mine. It's hard not to pose and preen and say my handful of lines a little louder than I should.

Seeing yourself as the main character doesn't make you a narcissist. If you're humble and shy, you're still usually the main character in an unfolding miniseries. It's just a miniseries about the challenges facing a humble, shy person. Even the most humble among us, the shyest among us, tend to focus inward on the inevitable centrality of our own experiences and our distorted, imperfect memories of our past.

Here's a different way to go through life.

To get at the alternative, think about an ensemble cast for a sitcom or a series. In a show like *Friends*, there's no star, no main character. There's just a bunch of people weaving in and out of one another's lives. The show may be called *Seinfeld*, but he's not the main character. There are four main characters. The show is about their relationships, not just the narrative arc of Jerry's life. Or think of the movie *Love Actually*. A star-studded cast but no one's the star of the movie. It's a story about love and connection, not the adventures of a central protagonist.

Or imagine going out on a dance floor with your partner. What is your attitude toward the dance? Perhaps it's to get as much as possible out of the experience for your own satisfaction. Your goal might be to attract attention to yourself and to impress people with your skills, to earn their applause and respect. You might think of the dance floor as primarily a place of competition where your goal is to outshine the other dancers and move up in the rankings. A lot of people dance through life like this, and it's not the worst attitude, as long as you don't try to trip up the other competitors.

Alternatively, you might choose to sublimate your own status or the ability to express yourself in hopes of making your partner shine, or to enhance the experience of all of the dancers out on the floor. You might focus on being part of something larger than yourself, weaving near and around the other dancers in unexpected and delightful ways.

When you act tactfully on the dance floor and behave properly, keeping others—your partner and the other couples—in mind, you have a choice in how to think of the experience before, during, and after. You can pride yourself on your selfless behavior or you can see yourself in a more holistic way, as part of something larger than yourself, a fuller, more connected experience.

We have a choice in how we perceive and frame our daily experiences. One choice is to see ourselves as fundamentally atomistic, heroic, and existentially lonely. The other is to see ourselves as connected and belonging to something, with that belonging at the center of the experience. How we frame the before, during, and after of our experiences changes how our daily experiences become part of us.

How would you live differently if you saw yourself as part of an ensemble rather than the main character? How would this ensemble idea work in practice?

Suppose I'm meeting someone for coffee, someone I haven't seen in a while. Looking ahead to the conversation, I catalog a few stories I hope to share—maybe a funny experience I had or a recent success. During the conversation, I spend a lot of time thinking about what I'm going to say next and to make sure I make my points. This is particularly likely to be my focus if it's a professional conversation rather than a chat with a friend. How can I make a good impression? What can I get this person to do for me?

But even when I'm with a friend, I can use my friend in direct and indirect ways for my own goals. After the conversation is over, I can savor having told the stories I wanted to tell and congratulate myself on how funny I was or how eloquent. This perspective is self-centered even if I am gracious enough to split the airtime in half and let my conversational partner talk as much as I do.

A different way to experience that conversation is to think of it not as alternating monologues but as an actual conversation, an emergent experience that goes in unexpected, unplanned directions. I can think of it as more of an improvisation, which is an organic art, than a scripted, prefab conversation.

Sure, when talking to a friend, I may have something to share that has happened to me recently and is important. But I don't want to focus on that to the exclusion of the rest of the experience. Don't go into the conversation with an itinerary. It's better to discover what you want to say through the process of conversation and not a pre-planned script.

Instead of savoring your conversational brilliance, savor the experience of interacting with another human being. See what happens without expectation during that encounter and without a plan to steer it in particular directions. Give your conversational partner your fullest attention without thinking of what you're going to say next.

Rather than <u>see your friends and family</u> as objects to serve your goals and increase your utility, see them as partners you commit to with no agenda as to what might emerge from interacting with them. View the chance to interact with them as more of an exploration and adventure than a scripted drama. Allow another human being the chance to open their heart. That can turn out to be a much more meaningful drama than the one where you're the main character, even if it means giving up control of the process.

Perceiving Friends & Family

In a way, all of this is just an obvious cliché—friends and <u>family make life meaningful.</u> So treat them well. We all know that. But if we know that, why do we glance down at our phone in the middle of a conversation with one of our children because we've received a notification or an alert? Why do we look over the shoulder of the person we're talking to at a party to see if there is someone more interesting, or worse, someone more useful to us in achieving some goal? Why do we often fail to make sufficient time to do things with our friends that offer no immediate benefit to us? Why do we let friends drift away and miss a chance to stay connected? Why do we check the caller ID and decide to ignore the call? We tell ourselves, They're family! They'll understand!

But most of all, why do we give in to our natural impulse and see ourselves as the main character? If we can see our life alongside friends and family and colleagues as more of an ensemble we are fortunate to be part of, we'll treat them better and even treat ourselves better. "Better" isn't really the right word. Daily life will have a different texture—one that is richer and more satisfying.

In *The Master and His Emissary*, psychiatrist Iain McGilchrist argues that the left side of the brain and the right side of the brain pay attention and process experience in different ways. Here is the way he describes the difference in his interview on my *EconTalk* podcast.

The left hemisphere is good at helping us manipulate the world, but not good at helping us to understand it. To just use this bit, and then that bit, and then that bit. But the right hemisphere has a kind of sustained, broad, vigilant attention instead of this narrow, focused, piecemeal attention. And it sustains a sense of being, a continuous being, in the world. So, these are very different *kinds* of attention.

He goes on to say that the right side of the brain is about connecting, and betweenness—the relationship between things that interact together. It sees the whole picture rather than the narrowest part. Of course we need both parts of the brain. But work on strengthening the part that feels connected, the part that yearns for connection. That's the part that's in the shadows, the part that's hard to remember.

Rabbi Jonathan Sacks wrote often about the difference between a contract and a covenant. With a contract, it's all about what's in it for me. In a contractual relationship, you keep score. You worry about being exploited. That makes for a bad marriage and a bad friendship.

A covenant, on the other hand, is a promise. A covenant says: we're together. Because of the commitment behind a covenant, you can afford to let your interactions with another person be free of making sure you get your "fair share." You can enjoy the ride. You keep commitments not out of fear that the other person will exploit you but because you want to be the kind of person whose commitments can be counted on. Sacks said that marriage turns love into loyalty. That commitment takes both parties beyond what's in it for me.

With a contract, it's easy to feel the other people aren't living up to their commitments at the level you expected. With a contract, you can easily imagine not renewing when the contract expires. It's just a transaction and maybe you can find a better deal somewhere else. But with a covenant, your friends and family aren't objects for you to exploit for more gain. They're partners on your journey through life.

Instead of wondering and worrying whether you are getting enough out of the relationship, you enjoy the shared experience. And if you are really lucky or work at it very hard, you privilege the principle of the covenant sufficiently so that sacrifices are no longer sacrifices. They may feel that way at first. But you can build a habit of partnership and turn a sacrifice into a satisfying habit. By reframing how we see our own lives—less as the story of a heroic figure and more of an ensemble—we can be better friends, better spouses, and more fully human.

It's surprisingly hard to do. But working at it liberates you from the pull of self. I suggest some ways to get better at it in the next chapter. Part of what the ensemble mind-set does is help you get over yourself. It makes you smaller, in a good way. Your ego shrinks to scale. You're not the center of the universe or the hero of some outsize set of stories you tell about yourself or even the star of the show. When you see yourself as part of an ensemble, you feel less outrage at things that once seemed unjust but that you now recognize as unimportant.

In the choir of life, don't be a diva. Lower your voice and revel in the harmony. On the dance floor of life, make room for the other dancers and let your partner shine. Try to be aware of your natural impulse to ask, what's in it for me, and make room instead for what the people around you need for the journey we're all in together.

A nontrivial part of this book is about the danger of focusing too narrowly on your personal satisfaction. Is that really so dangerous? Surely, you do have to look out for yourself. I'm just suggesting that what you really want is a little more complicated than it appears at first glance. If all you do is focus on yourself in the narrowest sense, you might miss something important in the shadows.

This is particularly true when we encounter the wild problem of an ethical dilemma that forces us to confront who we really are—what principles or values do we want to honor? What principles or values should we aspire to and how might we come to keep them rather than betray them? Facing an ethical dilemma forces us to think about what kind of person we truly are and who we might become. In the next chapter, I look at how an ethical dilemma can help us find a way to fight our narrowest utilitarian desires when they are in tension with our highest selves.

9

Privilege Your Principles

Ethical dilemmas are wild problems where the tension between the pig and the philosopher is front and center. What feels good in the moment has consequences that can compromise our sense of self and cost us in ways that persist over time. Narrow utilitarianism is often in tension with some higher principle related to flourishing.

For example, suppose you find a wallet lying on the ground. You pick it up and inside you find two hundred dollars in cash, along with a variety of credit cards and a driver's license. You look around. The street is deserted. You're alone. What should you do?

I posed the lost-wallet question during a Zoom seminar to about one hundred high school seniors studying economics at an elite private school. The response was nearly unanimous: the students thought that according to economics, it's rational to keep the wallet as long as no one saw you pick it up. They explained you could use the cash to buy whatever you liked and therefore you'd be better off. Because no one saw you, the students saw no cost in loss of reputation from pocketing the money or fear of being accosted for failing to try to find the owner. In their eyes, keeping the wallet and spending the money were desirable and feasible and so completely rational in the economist's calculus.

Rational
Decision

The economist Ariel Rubinstein defines a rational decision:

1. The person asks, What is desirable?

2. The person asks, What is feasible?

3. The person chooses the most desirable from among the feasible alternatives.

This seems beyond reproach. What could be more obvious? The students certainly agreed.

The standard critique of this model of human behavior is that we are flawed calculators—we act inconsistently; we are fooled by uncertainty; we have biases. This is the world of behavioral economics. But the deeper problem is that if we're not careful, when we think of what is desirable, we will think about the pool and the margarita and not so much about flourishing.

This is surely the narrowest form of utilitarianism and unfortunately some economists encourage such thinking in the teaching of economics and in their research. They confuse what we want to do in our narrow self-interest with what we ought to do. They are not the same thing.

The students ignored the possibility that if helping someone else gives you pleasure (and clearly many people do in fact enjoy helping others), then returning the wallet might be rational by the economist's definition. The pleasure you get from pleasing the owner of the wallet can be larger than the pleasure you receive from spending the money.

And there is a third kind of person—a person who wants to keep the wallet but returns it anyway, because it's the right thing to do. This person believes that the goal of life isn't simply to milk our experience for the maximum amount of pleasure over pain. Sometimes you do the right thing simply because you think you should. And you feel miserable making that sacrifice. You make the sacrifice anyway because you aspire to be a certain kind of person. You have a desire to be an honest person.

If you don't have any feelings about the right thing to do, returning the wallet or keeping it isn't a wild problem at all—you simply try to measure the gains from the money against the costs to your reputation if you're caught. But if you think returning the wallet is the right thing to do, or you have an inkling that it's the right thing to do, narrow utilitarian considerations conflict with how you see yourself and your sense of self. How should you choose in this situation?

A few summers ago, my wife and I spent four days at a lodge in the Grand Tetons. On the third day, my wife realized she had lost one of the diamond earrings I'd given her as an anniversary present years before. We looked all over the room. We called the place where we'd gone rafting that day. Nothing. I tried to comfort my wife—we can replace it; it's not a tragedy. But I could see it weighed on her.

The next morning, we had to switch rooms—the room

we started in had been available for only the first part of our stay. We headed out for a long hike. The vistas were amazing. We saw a moose. We saw a grizzly bear on the mountain across the river. It was a long, exhausting, rewarding day. When we got back to the lodge, we headed to our new room. When we arrived, we found a note on the bedside table: "I found this in room 901. I don't know if it is yours. —Teodora."

"This" was my wife's diamond earring sitting serenely on top of the note. Room 901 was the room we had been in before. The housekeeper had found the earring on the floor while cleaning the room we had vacated. She was smart enough or maybe hopeful enough to realize that perhaps it had been lost by an earlier guest and not by my wife. Maybe it didn't belong to us. Maybe Teodora could claim it as her own if we told her that we hadn't lost it.

Sometimes I imagine Teodora that morning, doing her job. Did she like it? Hate it? What is it like, day after summer day, sweeping, vacuuming, dusting, wiping down surfaces with the majestic Grand Tetons constantly visible and large enough that you feel you can reach out and touch them? Maybe the work is drudgery. Or maybe cleaning for her has a meditative aspect as she focuses on her task. Or maybe her mind is elsewhere. She sees something sparkle at her feet. She bends down to take a closer look. Is that a piece of glass or something else?

What is her first thought when she sees that it's a diamond earring? Excitement? Joy? Temptation? She was alone in the room. No one was watching. A religious person might think of God watching. But even if Teodora did not believe in God, she knew that someone was indeed watching—Teodora. How did she react to her discovery? What emotions surged through her?

How easy it would have been to drop such a tiny object into her pocket. Maybe she even put the diamond there to see what it would feel like, toying with the idea of keeping it. Maybe she went on with her cleaning, thinking over what to do. Did her decision depend on how big the diamond was? Is there a trade-off between honesty and money? Is there a case where honesty becomes too expensive because of what you have to sacrifice?

Teodora was a summer employee from another country. A job in a resort is usually not that high-paying—some of her reward surely came in the form of the mountains she enjoyed seeing every day and the hiking nearby that she could enjoy on her days off. She could easily have justified pocketing the earring on the grounds that any guest in the lodge would surely have a standard of living higher than hers. She could have convinced herself that we had no way of identifying the diamond and she could just as easily believe it had come from some unfindable past guest. But she didn't. She wrote the note. She placed the diamond earring on top of the note.

The next day, my wife tracked down Teodora, hugged her, thanked her in tears, and gave her an unasked-for reward of what my wife and I remember to be fifty dollars. Do you think Teodora returned the diamond earring because she anticipated the hug or the reward? I don't think so.

I think Teodora returned the diamond earring because she saw herself as an honest person, the kind of person who returns a lost object regardless of its value. The kind of person who does the right thing. Had she kept the earring, Teodora would have felt as if she had betrayed herself.

I didn't speak to her about it, but I suspect she didn't think about the worth of the diamond relative to her desire to do the right thing and maintain her self-respect as an honest person. She put her sense of self first; there was no trade-off, no list of expected costs and benefits. Maybe no matter the size of the diamond, she intended to do the right thing.

How do you feel when you hear about someone like Teodora, someone who does the right thing even though they pay a price? Do you think Teodora is a fool for returning the earring, duped by religion or the lessons her parents may have imparted to her? Is it sensible to give up what could have been a very pleasant windfall and pass it on to a much richer person? Do you respect or pity Teodora, who made sure that a guest had a vacation unmarred by the loss of a sentimental (and valuable) object? Is Teodora a sucker or a saint?

In the standard tool kit of the economist, the utilitarian view, Teodora returned the diamond because the pleasure she received from doing what she saw as the right thing was greater to her than the value of the diamond. In the economist's view of the world, every person has their price—an amount of money or other benefit they would be willing to accept to violate their principles. This is a powerful insight that can help us think about the flaws of our fellow human beings and our own flaws.

It is certainly the case that people struggle to live up to their principles when keeping those principles is expensive. One of my favorite summaries of this idea is the expression "where you stand depends on where you sit." Another version was uttered, if not originated, by Upton Sinclair: "It is difficult to get a man to understand something, when his salary depends upon his not understanding it." If you are self-aware, you realize that monetary and nonmonetary rewards and punishments do exert pressure on you to behave in certain ways. Economists exploit this reality when designing incentive structures— subsidies and taxes, for example—that encourage or discourage certain kinds of behavior.

In an often told story that is probably apocryphal, the British playwright George Bernard Shaw asks a beautiful woman at a dinner party if she would be willing to go home with him for the night in exchange for one million British pounds. She admits that she would think about it. OK, he responds, how about ten pounds? What do you take me for? she asks, insulted. We've already established that, he responds, we're just talking price.

In my experience, when you suggest to people that they respond to incentives, which is another way of saying that they take trade-offs into account when making choices, they get very angry. They don't like the idea that they can be bought by a subsidy or a big enough payoff. Most people will indeed buy more of something when the price is lowered or less of something when it gets more expensive. So why are they offended?

They're offended because, like the woman at the dinner party with George Bernard Shaw, they like to think that their principles, their core values, are not for sale. We are more than calculating machines that recalibrate when the prices change. Yes, real human beings will sacrifice their principles if the price is right. But the anger that people feel when confronted with the possibility that such an insight might apply to them is understandable. We don't like to think that our virtue has a price. Of course sometimes it does. Sometimes we sell ourselves, and cheaply. But that's a flaw, not a virtue to be praised merely because it seems to be rational.

When it comes to decisions when your essence is on the line, don't consider the cost. Save your sense of self. Return the diamond, no matter how large. No trade-offs. Rationality, narrowly defined, says consider the cost. Teodora's teaching is simpler. Do the right thing. Return the diamond. Don't consider the cost of returning the diamond, the things you might have enjoyed with the money if you sold it.

Benjamin Franklin's advice when making a decision was to list the pluses and minuses and find items on either side of the ledger that you could cancel out. It's just a way of figuring out which solution is likely to lead to the most satisfaction. But Teodora teaches us something simpler. Nothing cancels out betraying who you are or who you aspire to be. So you can't add "losing respect for myself" as one of the costs of keeping the diamond. Well, you can, but it's silly because it's the one factor that nothing else cancels out.

When Darwin rejected the calculus of his pluses and minuses and wrote "Marry—Marry—Marry," he was recognizing that the decision to become a husband is about more than just the day-to-day pleasures of being married or being a father. When Persi Diaconis talks about what we are "really after," when Phoebe Ellsworth writes about what we "really want," when Piet Hein in his poem talks about what we really are hoping for, they're all

143

tapping into something other than how we feel about the costs and benefits. They're talking about who we are, our essence, and not just the daily experiences of life.

Economics does recognize that there might be some things that we pursue before we consider other choices. We say such preferences are "lexicographic." So yes, we can squeeze prioritizing our sense of self, our dignity, into the economist's model of rational choice. But it's just a way of really saying it's outside the model.

We can imagine cases where the utilitarian costs and benefits are so large that there comes a point where sense of self is trumped. If Teodora had a child who needed an operation that she couldn't afford, I could imagine her keeping the diamond even though she would feel guilty. We would not judge her harshly. If anything, that's the exception that proves the rule—Teodora's identity as a mother would be another principle at her core competing with honesty. She would put either of those principles ahead of narrow utilitarianism.

And as I said about my decision to move to Israel to become president of Shalem College, if it meant living in a rat-ridden hovel and having inadequate nutrition in order to do the job, the fact that it seemed like a calling probably wouldn't have been enough to get me to move. But these are the extreme cases that one easily recognizes as the exceptions that prove the rule.

The rule is simple: **Privilege your principles.** ← *The rule*

Your decisions define who you are. Don't make trade-offs when it comes to your essence. Live with integrity. Do the right thing and respect yourself. That at least should be the starting place. For Teodora, the principle was honesty. Sometimes principles conflict. There could be more important principles—the love of a child—that might push honesty aside.

Putting your principles above the day-to-day costs and benefits is about more than ethics or the virtue of honesty that we confront when we find a lost wallet or are offered a consulting opportunity that is highly lucrative but ethically questionable. Privileging your principles is about what kind of person you want to be and who you might want to become. It's about visiting a friend in the hospital when it feels like you have better things to do. It's about listening to that friend who needs to share something even though you're in a hurry to run an errand that you're itching to finish. It's about voting when you're dreading the wait in line.

There are two virtues of putting your principles—whatever you feel defines who you really are—above narrower costs and benefits from your decisions.

The first is the virtue of simplicity. Having a rule that you always put your principles above the narrower costs and benefits means you spend less time deliberating and suffering. You have a rule. You try to follow the rule. You may struggle to follow the rule, but the rule is the default. So in principle, you don't agonize over whether following the rule is too costly or not in this particular case. You just follow the rule.

The rule might be "I am the kind of person who always returns lost objects to their owners." Or "I am the kind of person who visits a friend when they are in the hospital." Or "I am the kind of person who attends the funeral of a friend, even if it interferes with my work." (And they almost always do, don't they? Go anyway.)

In the case of marriage, you might have a set of rules like these: "I am the kind of person who is loyal to my spouse." Or "I am the kind of person who doesn't make jokes about my spouse in front of other people even when they're incredibly funny." Or "I am the kind of person who doesn't lash out at my spouse in public even when it sure feels like they deserve it based on how my spouse treated me yesterday." Sometimes it's hard to keep the rules. But they are the ideal and what to strive toward.

Surely, in many situations, rules are an unnecessary straitjacket, though, right? Wouldn't it be better to treat each fork in the road rationally, weighing all the costs and benefits? Surely keeping blunt rules without exception means giving up satisfactions that I might otherwise enjoy.

For most of us, that counterpoint misunderstands how we actually behave in keeping to what we believe in and want to accomplish.

Yes, rules are nice because they reduce time deliberating and trying to measure those pesky, hard-to-measure costs and benefits. But rules have a much more important advantage over what seems to be the rational approach of going case by case and trying to calculate and weigh the costs and benefits more thoroughly. Rules prevent us from fooling ourselves.

My wife and I currently live in an apartment in Jerusalem on the third floor. There are stairs and an elevator to choose from. When I arrived, I decided to have a rule—always take the stairs. I spend most of my day in front of a keyboard. Exercise, even a little bit, is good for me.

I could have had a more "rational" rule—take the stairs unless I'm carrying a lot of things. Or take the stairs unless it's really hot out. Because of course there are days that are so hot and I'm carrying so many groceries that it's silly to take the stairs. For those extreme cases, the imagined future health benefits of the exercise from taking the stairs are outweighed by the pain of climbing them on such a hot day with so much stuff.

But I know myself. If instead of having a rule, each time I come to the door I have to decide whether to take the elevator or the stairs, I will often find ways to justify using the elevator. I will effortlessly rationalize the decision—I slept poorly last night so it's OK to take the elevator this time; it's a bit warm today, isn't it?; I am carrying an extra book in my backpack—and I will end up taking the elevator more often than my better self would like. My lesser self, the one I am rather than the one I want to be, will find a way to justify skipping the stairs.

Benjamin Franklin understood this well. He wrote in his *Autobiography*, "So convenient a thing it is to be a *reasonable Creature*, since it enables one to find or make a Reason for every thing one has a mind to do." So use rules. When narrow utilitarianism conflicts with flourishing, remember that the pool is what you know and the pool is seductive. Work hard to remember what your principles are and privilege them—put them first unless you have a strong reason not to.

Rules are useful in maintaining who we are, our sense of self. But they're probably even more important in helping us become who we might want to become. You may not have any principles to privilege but perhaps you can acquire some.

Rubinstein's (and the mainstream economist's) definition of a rational choice assumes that what we desire is fixed—what are called "stable preferences" in economics. But as the philosopher Harry Frankfurt points out, we human beings are the only animals that have desires about our desires. So if you don't have a conscience and no one is watching you, keeping the wallet is rational. But maybe you are ashamed of that feeling. Maybe, because you would like to contribute to your community instead of exploiting it, you aspire to have a conscience.

As Agnes Callard writes in her book *Aspiration,* life isn't just about who we are but who we aspire to be. Right now, I may not care for opera. But I might aspire to appreciate it. But aspiration is about more than our tastes in exotic food or learning to love opera. I might aspire to be a better person than I am now. I might aspire to be a more reliable friend. A better parent. A more loving spouse or partner. A kinder, more patient person when I interact with strangers. More honorable. We can choose these paths or at least seek to discover them, if we find them worthy.

Economists once saw human beings as more than just maximizing machines that take account only of costs and benefits. Frank Knight, a Chicago economist from the first half of the twentieth century, said that the human creature is an "aspiring rather than a desiring being." His student and economics Nobel laureate James Buchanan contrasted the natural human being with what he called "artifactual man," people who craft themselves. Buchanan, speaking of human aspiration, wrote, "Man wants freedom to become the man he wants to become." We are in the process of becoming. So give some thought as to what you desire to desire.

If you don't have a conscience, how do you get one? You might desire to feel bad about keeping the wallet, but if you don't feel bad, now what?

→ Max Beerbohm, a writer at the turn of the twentieth century, suggests a way forward in his story "The Happy Hypocrite." A wicked man, very much a shameless hedonist, George Hell, falls head over heels for a virtuous, beautiful woman, Jenny Mere. He proposes marriage, but she explains that she could never love anyone other than someone with the face of a saint. Hell is out of luck there. So he pays a magical mask maker for a lifelike mask that will make him look saintly and loving.

Wearing the mask, he pursues the woman and wins her heart and hand. When they go to get the marriage license, Hell struggles with his deception—he sees himself as a dishonest trickster. He decides to give himself a new name, and enters George Heaven on the marriage license.

Under the spell of love and remorseful about his past, Hell, now Heaven, decides to atone. He gives up his wicked ways. One month into the marriage, Hell's jilted lover—a woman known as La Gambogi—plots revenge. She knows about the mask and the true essence of the man who lies beneath the mask. In front of his new bride, La Gambogi tears the mask off George Heaven's face, exposing the Hell he really is.

As the reader, we know what's going to happen. The good woman will be confronted with the true face of George Hell, the face of a man of appetite, a pursuer of pleasure, a man without virtue. A sinner rather than the saint he appears to be, George Hell will be revealed as a hypocrite. The wife will recoil in horror. Their marriage will fall apart.

But Beerbohm surprises us. Once the mask has been removed, La Gambogi discovers, as do George and his new wife, that the face beneath the mask now matches what the mask displayed to the world—the face of a saint. The inner man now matches the outer one. Hell has become Heaven. He no longer needs the mask. Cast aside, the magic mask made of wax melts in the sun.

And so the story ends. What is the lesson?

George Hell is the moral equivalent of a vampire. He wants to become an anti-vampire, George Heaven. He desires to have different desires than he once had. How is that possible? The answer is practice. Through love and changed behavior, Hell does more than change who he appears to be. He changes who he actually is.

To get to where he wants to go, he wears the mask. We generally don't like hypocrisy—the betrayal of principle—

but Beerbohm casts it as a virtue. By pretending to be good and going through the motions, George Hell transforms himself. He repairs his hypocrisy, not by removing the mask but by removing his flaws. And he becomes that better person by acting against his core principles as a shameless hedonist. He tricks his bride but in doing so, by performing the actions of a good person, he becomes that person. His old self melts away the same way his mask does in the sun. And so does his hypocrisy. With the actions of goodness, his inner self and outer self no longer clash.

The mask forces George Hell to go against his narrow utilitarian self, to live up to who he aspires to be. Frank Knight wrote, "Insofar as man is wise or good, his 'character' is acquired chiefly by posing as better than he is, until a part of his pretense becomes a habit."

Practice may not make perfect, but done correctly it should lead to better.

So practice at what you want to become. You can change your preferences. What once appealed to you can become unappealing. What you once found unappealing can potentially give you pleasure if you try it and persist at it. Goodness is an acquired taste. And habits are exactly that, habits. If you come to enjoy being generous, honest, less self-centered, the habit becomes self-enforcing, as Frank Knight suggested.

When I introduced the question of the lost wallet at the start of this chapter, I described three types of people: a person without a conscience, a person with a conscience who gets pleasure from doing the right thing, and a third kind of person—a person without a conscience who'd like to develop one. "The Happy Hypocrite" suggests that you can develop that conscience and, after having done so, transform yourself into a person who actually does the right thing out of self-interest—doing good becomes a source of pleasure.

The seventeenth-century French writer La Rochefoucauld wrote, "Virtues are swallowed up by self-interest as rivers are lost in the sea." The philosopher and economist Dan Klein argues that what La Rochefoucauld meant was that there is a way to make practicing a virtue self-interested. That way, Teodora enjoys doing the right thing and doesn't even see it as a sacrifice. I don't believe her discovery and returning of the diamond earring was her first rodeo when it came to doing the right thing. Her parents, maybe the friends she chose to be around, maybe her religion, grooved the habit of honesty and empathy.

In chapter 6, I mentioned the documentary filmmaker Penny Lane who donated a kidney to a stranger when she realized that the costs to her were so much smaller than the benefits to the recipient. I spoke to Lane about her decision—it wasn't that she looked forward to a lifetime of patting herself on the back and feeling good about herself. It was simply that she thought the moral calculus was open and shut.

What was even more interesting was her answer to how the experience had changed her. Just like carrying around a robot baby that wakes you up multiple times in the middle of the night isn't the same as becoming a parent, I suspected that donating a kidney is about more than an arduous set of tests and surgery and leaving the hospital with one less kidney than when you were admitted. How had donating changed Lane's sense of herself? Her answer was that if you had asked her before the donation if she was generous, giving, altruistic, she would have said no. And now she said, "I feel like I am." She added, "If you think of yourself as an altruistic person, you become more generous and giving." Max Beerbohm would be proud.

There is a much-repeated story on the internet, usually told about a Native American elder. Here is Eliot Rosen's version from his book *Experiencing the Soul*.

> A Native American Elder once described his own inner struggles in this manner: "Inside of me there are two dogs. One of the dogs is mean and evil. The other dog is good. The mean dog fights the good dog all the time." When asked which dog wins, he reflected for a moment and replied, "The one I feed the most."

Great Quote

In most areas of life, especially the important ones, our desires aren't fixed in the way economists usually think of them. Many of our desires are in conflict. We all have urges that we long to indulge and sometimes these urges sit uneasily with us. Sometimes we long to limit our urges, whether food, sex, money, or the app on your phone that you spend time with compulsively. We have a good dog and a bad one fighting each other all the time. Feed the good dog. Feed it often enough and it starts to win the fights with the bad dog.

10

Be Like Bill

One reason wild problems are so unpleasant is that the future is shrouded from us. Because we crave control and certainty, our natural impulse is to try to illuminate the darkness with more information and better strategies for coping with wild problems. This is a fool's game, an illusion. You're better off trying to get used to the darkness.

That sounds good, but let's be honest: Most of us aren't bats. We don't like darkness. Telling a human being to get used to the darkness goes against our nature. Certainty makes our hearts sing; uncertainty makes us anxious. Telling yourself rationally that the future is unknowable isn't that helpful. That pit in your stomach doesn't go away even if your mind says it's irrational to fear the future. Your mind is particularly poor at controlling what your stomach is telling you.

In this chapter and the next one, I present two meta-strategies for dealing with the uncertainty of the future and the challenge of wild problems. The first comes from an unlikely source, Bill Belichick, the head coach of the New England Patriots. Belichick has earned six Super Bowl rings as a head coach. He's widely considered a genius, a mastermind, the Einstein of the NFL. Ironically, being like Bill means finding a way to cope with how little you know.

Every year at the NFL Draft, teams pick college players in reverse order to how the teams finished in the previous season. Belichick and his staff, like with every NFL team, spend hundreds of hours preparing. Teams have extensive data on hundreds of players. They conduct personal interviews with dozens of their top prospects. They watch hundreds if not thousands of hours of film that show the players' college performances. The Patriots, like all NFL teams, use this mix of qualitative and quantitative information to grade prospects, rank them, and make their draft picks accordingly.

This system is so complicated and important to the future of the team that any video footage of the Patriots' war rooms blurs out the whiteboards in the background so competitors get no clue about the system the Patriots use to make their choices.

But here's the funny thing. The Patriots don't really believe in their system as a reliable predictor. They know that their knowledge about the future viability of current college players is loose, vague, and indeterminate. We know that because Belichick is famous for his eagerness to trade a draft pick from an earlier round for multiple draft picks in later rounds. He seems to value quantity over quality. He rarely gives up multiple picks to move up in the draft to choose a particular player—he knows that no matter how many signs point to a player being successful in the NFL, an enormous amount of uncertainty surrounds any one individual.

So what Belichick does is worry less about getting the exact right player with any one pick. Instead, he tries to choose lots of players. That would seem impossible—each team gets the same number of draft picks. But the Patriots often have more picks than other teams because of Bill's willingness to trade a high draft pick for more than one pick in a later round. Once the players he chooses arrive at training camp, Belichick gets a lot more information, and in particular, information that he can't glean from film or talking to college coaches or data gathered at the NFL Scouting Combine, the arduous set of speed, agility, strength, and intelligence tests.

The preseason lets Belichick find out not just whether a player is skilled but how those skills will fit into the Patriots' system. He finds out how the player's personality (which is impossible to observe from a distance) will mesh with those of other players on the team and the expectations of the Patriots' staff. One might be tempted to assume that a good player is a good player and a bad one is a bad one. But the Patriots often get strong production from a player that other teams couldn't generate. And some players perform well elsewhere but play poorly in the Patriots' system.

Belichick knows that only a fraction of the players he chooses will thrive in his system. But he also knows how hard it is to know in advance which players will turn out well. So rather than focusing all of his energy on making better decisions on Draft Day, he increases the denominator, the total number of picks. Belichick embraces his ignorance. He understands he doesn't have a guidebook to Rome. He learns as he goes along.

The players who don't fit in are cut. Belichick doesn't seem to care about whether they were high draft picks or low ones. He also signs a lot of players after the draft— the contracts for undrafted players are particularly inexpensive. And for the last eighteen years, an undrafted free agent, and sometimes more than one, makes the team.

What can we learn from Bill Belichick?

Other than the unappreciated value of a first-rate long snapper, the history of lacrosse at the United States Naval Academy, and the unappreciated value of players who can play multiple positions (all things that Bill Belichick is obsessed with and a world authority on, among a very small group of similarly interested devotees), we can learn at least four lessons from Bill that extend beyond sports.

1. Optionality is powerful.

Optionality is when you have the freedom to do something but not the obligation. Think of Zappos. Zappos is the shoe website with free shipping and free returns. We all understand the pleasantness of not having to pay for shipping or returns. It's not exactly free—it means the prices are probably going to be a little bit higher than they might otherwise be. In return (sorry!), you get optionality, the ability to change your mind once you've seen the shoes up close and worn them around the house. They may look comfortable. They might have a 4.97 out of 5 rating with thousands of positive reviews. But until you've put them on, you can't know whether they'll be comfortable for you. Being able to return them without charge (and at a relatively low level of hassle) gives you optionality. You buy the shoes without obligation to keep them.

Optionality doesn't just mean a lower cost from a mistake because you don't have to pay for shipping. It should change your whole process of shopping. Buy more shoes (assuming you have a credit card that isn't maxed out). Don't agonize over whether they're the right choice. Don't waste time trying to get more information about whether the reviewers who liked the shoes are like you (do people with narrow feet like these shoes?) or whether the reviews at Zappos are reliable.

Shop more, worry less. I'm guessing Belichick likes Zappos because free returns and free shipping fit his draft philosophy. Because he knows he can cut a player who doesn't fit without making a long-term commitment, he orders more players rather than trying to find out in advance with any certainty who the best ones are. He sleeps better around the draft because he knows he has something like the law of large numbers working in his favor—with a big enough class of rookies, some of them will work out when tested in the preseason.

Inevitably, Belichick (and every other NFL brain trust that faces the uncertainty of the draft) neglects to pick players who are available only to discover in the coming years that he missed out on a superstar. I suspect he tries at some level to figure out what he might have been able to see that would have identified those players at draft time. But I also suspect he knows that much of what makes those players great simply can't be seen in advance. I'm sure he tries to make his draft analysis better every year. But there is a fundamental uncertainty around the process. Rather than trying to perfect his draft analysis, he looks for strategies to cope with the inevitable uncertainty. He spends more time getting used to the darkness and less time looking to expand the light.

The essence of optionality is appreciating that you can't

know in advance what will work. It's the same idea behind venture capital. Even the best venture capitalists strike out seven times out of ten. One time out of ten they might hit what's called a unicorn—a company that turns out to have a valuation of a billion dollars or more. Why can't they figure out the unicorns in advance and just invest in those? They can't. Investing is a wild problem. Venture capitalists rely on the law of large numbers. They let the market decide which of their ten investments is a home run. They can't do any better than that.

Use this idea for living. Try to have more experiences than fewer. Try stuff. Stop doing the stuff that isn't for you. Embrace the opportunities that make your heart sing. Spend less time trying to figure out in advance what those might be and more time taking chances as long as you can opt out at a low enough cost. Exploring can turn out much better than a planned itinerary.

The advantages of optionality are a double-edged sword for many of us. We fear making a decision so we want more information. So we date someone for an extended period of time telling ourselves we are doing so just to make sure this is the right person. But there is also an argument for getting more information about someone you have not met. Dating lots of different people also gives you more information about yourself and how you interact with a potential partner and raises your chances of identifying someone you like who likes you. There is no easy way to deal with this trade-off but perhaps it is helpful to be aware of the reality that many times the delay in making a decision is not simply because we don't have information. We delay because we don't like making decisions.

2. Don't assume that what works for them works for you. When you can, put the shoes on. Test-drive the car.

Surveys asking people about their level of happiness may not apply to you, your tastes, your passions, and most important, who you become over time. Putting the shoes on tells you a lot more than reading about how comfortable the shoes are. Seeing the player at your practice rather than someone else's is particularly valuable. Test-drive the car. Not every wild problem is really a vampire problem, with no hope of return if you get cold feet. Don't be intimidated by what's at stake.

3. Sunk costs are sunk.

Belichick doesn't seem to be embarrassed to admit that a decision he made didn't work out. He's OK with admitting that the draft isn't much of a science and more of a roll of the dice. He tries out the player. If the shoe doesn't fit, he doesn't feel compelled to wear it because people might lose respect for his judgment. The opposite is the case—he moves on from a player (and not just with draft picks) because he understands that some decisions inevitably turn out differently from what we expected. We're only human.

These aren't mistakes

Often in such situations, we'll say, I took the job, but it was a mistake. I got engaged, but it was a mistake. I went to law school, but it was a mistake. But none of those things are mistakes. A mistake is when you know you don't like anchovies but you keep ordering them on your pizza. A mistake is trusting someone you know is a person without honor.

Hope

Life choices that turn out differently from what we hoped aren't mistakes. They're just choices that turned out differently than we hoped. We shouldn't call those mistakes. You shouldn't beat yourself up over them. Forgive yourself. Wild problems that don't turn out well aren't mistakes. They're more like adventures. Adventures have twists and turns and ups and downs. Belichick teaches us that if you can go on an adventure that you can end without great cost, go. If it turns out badly, cut it short. If it turns out well, enjoy the ride. This beats trying to figure out in advance with any precision which adventures are the best ones.

4. Grit and persistence are overrated.

Yes, it's a bad idea to quit immediately just because something is difficult or a little unpleasant. Yes, some tastes are acquired tastes, but some things never become delightful. If you hated law school and hate being a lawyer, try a different kind of law. If that doesn't help, there's no shame in changing careers. If you hate law and leave it behind, don't say you made a mistake. How can it be a mistake when *Change* your information was so incomplete? When life turns out to be different than you thought it would be, or you turn out differently than you thought you'd like to be, change.

If you don't like being a vampire, take off the cape and enjoy the sunshine. Cut your losses and move on. Life's too short to stick mindlessly with things you discover aren't for you. Live. Change. Be like Bill.

Take advantage of optionality when you can. Some optionality is obvious—date before you marry. Be an intern before you join a company. Hire an intern before you make a long-term commitment to an employee. Visit a place before you move there. Don't finish every book you start.

Most decisions in life aren't literally vampire problems where once you've made a choice, there's no going back, no return. If you move to Israel and hate it, you can move somewhere else. If you marry badly, you can divorce, although I think marriage is one example of where grit and persistence might be underrated—work at making it better until you find that you can't. If you don't marry and you miss the human connection that a spouse brings, there are other ways to find connection and friendship. If you go to law school and you find you hate being a lawyer, you're not alone. If you stick with it anyway because you were told that persistence and grit are a virtue, you're also not alone. But the fact is that you're free to change your career, even when you've been a lawyer for a while.

A lot of what makes wild problems so painful is the specter of regret. You decide not to marry someone and you end up regretting it. Or the opposite—you marry someone and it doesn't turn out well. You go to law school and you hate it. The potential for these decisions to turn out badly tends to cause fear of making any decision at all. We say to ourselves that we need more time to gather information, ignoring that more information isn't going to help—it's just a form of procrastination.

Rabbi Jonathan Sacks said, "The only way to understand marriage is to get married. The only way to understand whether a certain career path is right for you is to actually try it for an extended period. Those who hover on the edge of a commitment, reluctant to make a decision until all the facts are in, will eventually find that life has passed them by. The only way to understand a way of life is to take the risk of living it." All the facts are never in.

One way to avoid letting life pass you by is to stop worrying about making a "mistake." It's not a mistake when you can't do any better. So spend less time on figuring out the "right" decision and more time on thinking about how to widen your options and how to cope with disappointment if the decision turns out badly. I think Bill Belichick sleeps well the night after the NFL draft. You can sleep well, too.

11

Live Like an Artist

William Faulkner once described writing a book as getting "the character in your mind. Once he is in your mind, and he is right, and he's true, then he does the work himself. All you need to do then is to trot along behind him and put down what he does and what he says." Unlike some novelists, Faulkner was claiming he didn't know how his book was going to turn out when he started. The characters he created and the situations he put them in took on a life of their own. There was an organic aspect to the process that defied the usual way we think of a genius at work, executing a brilliant plan to realize the vision. The vision emerges alongside the work. It isn't prefabricated.

Some people have the good luck (or maybe it's a curse) to have a prefab career or a prefab life. They know what they want or at least they think they do. They want to be a doctor, say. They're premed in college; they work hard and get good grades, are accepted at a respected medical school, secure a decent residency, and spend their life as a doctor. There's a lot to be said for that kind of focused plan. It can mean an incredibly rewarding career, both financially and psychologically.

But most of us don't have a prefab career or life. We don't know what we want. We find ourselves in Rome, with little or no idea of what exactly is best for us to do. What we want, what we enjoy, what gives our lives meaning, emerges from the choices we make, and that emergence takes place alongside the choices and what we learn from living with those choices, adjusting what we do accordingly. We figure out what we want not from studying it from our armchair or by looking it up in a book or consulting experts but from actual day-to-day experience. And until we have that day-to-day experience, and until we feel what it's like to put on a particular identity, we don't have a goal in the usual sense of that word.

We may try to craft our narrative the way a person knows that they want to be a doctor and then takes all the steps to make the plot turn out the way they planned. But for most of us, the plot isn't totally under our control. The narrative takes its own course. There are unexpected plot twists; characters drop out of the script and others show up unexpectedly.

Living like an artist is not a bad way to think about how to face a wild problem.

A villanelle is a French verse form consisting of five three-line stanzas and a final quatrain, with the first and third lines of the first stanza repeating alternately in the following stanzas. Elizabeth Bishop's poem "One Art" is widely considered one of the finest villanelles ever written. One poet, Sharon Bryan, argues that it is a "perfect mesh of form and content" and that if the villanelle were an athlete, it should have its jersey number retired because nothing could top Bishop's achievement.

Yet it took seventeen (!) drafts to produce that perfection. The poem emerged through the process of creation. A writer who goes simply by Beth at her blog, *Bluedragonfly10*, suggests that the poem itself made demands on Bishop on how it would be structured, particularly when already in draft number two the opening line, "the art of losing isn't hard to master," appears for the first time and gets repeated, suggesting a villanelle might be coming.

The fact that the poem became a villanelle so soon in its birth makes me believe that a poem has a form it is called to. This poem wanted to be a villanelle. A poem welcomes certain forms and dislikes others. This means that a poem has a life of its own, its own mind, its own voice, its own likes and dislikes just like a person does. And that means all art does. Art wants to be created in a way that welcomes in all the possibilities of its existence.

How can a poem "want" something or have a life of its own? Can't the poet write whatever she wants? Of course she can. But at some point, the poem is alive. Certain changes are no longer possible without starting from scratch. Other changes show up serendipitously, feel right, and are kept.

Can we think about the story of our life in this way?

Can we think of our lives as something we craft with an understanding that the result is not completely and sometimes hardly at all under our control?

We think of things that are not under our control as out of control, like some crazy amusement park ride where we have no idea of what's coming around the next turn. But recognizing that you are not in control doesn't mean there's no control at all or zero planning. It means trusting the opportunity to adjust the plan or journey to the new information that you learn as you go through the experience. It's like a week in Rome without a guidebook. It's like when you go into a skid on an icy road. Your natural reaction is to reclaim control of the car and turn the wheel back toward where you want to go or hit the brakes hard. But those actions usually make the skid worse. Sometimes it's better to simply take your foot off the gas and let the car regain its footing on its own.

Living like an artist means being open to discovery about the world and about yourself. As educator Lorne Buchman explores in his book *Make to Know*, poets, sculptors, novelists, and composers learn about what they are crafting in the process of crafting it. They don't start with an algorithm unless you consider "remove all the marble that isn't David" an algorithm for Michelangelo. Or "pick the right note that belongs after the ones that came before" as Beethoven seems to have proceeded.

Artists often have no idea what they're going to create. They make art in order to know what they are planning. Buchman quotes Picasso: "To know what you're going to draw, you have to begin drawing." Elizabeth Bishop discovered what she wanted to say in the process of saying it. So it is with life.

One practical aspect of living like an artist ties in with optionality. One of the best pieces of advice I've ever heard is the importance of saying no. If you're not careful, you'll find yourself bogged down by too many commitments, wasting time on trivial tasks and failing to achieve what you care most about. You won't be able to realize your plans—you're always getting sidetracked.

It's also one of the worst pieces of advice—if you always or too often say no, you'll miss a chance to connect with someone you will be glad to know, to discover something special or, even better, something precious. You'll reduce the amount of serendipity in your life. Taking advantage of optionality means saying yes to things that are not obviously worth doing but have the chance to expand your horizons, your experiences, your connections. And by doing so you will learn not just about opportunities but about yourself—what you like and what you find meaningful.

I may not be typical. If you want to be a doctor, you usually do need a plan and a way to get there from here. It's OK to have a plan, maybe even a lot more than OK. The hard part is knowing when to give up on the plan when things go sideways or you discover your plan isn't the right one for you. This is also an art. Some people will tell you: Never give up on your dreams! Persevere! But in fact you will discover that some dreams are unrealistic. Some dreams turn out to be nightmares that you should walk away from.

To know when to fold 'em and when to hold 'em is an art that is quantifiable in poker but not in life. Better to learn who you are—your strengths and limitations—and make each decision as best you can. Here is a case where having a rule—"always persevere," or "quit when it gets too hard"—will lead you astray. In life, knowing when to persevere and when to quit is a craft to cultivate.

Most of my proudest accomplishments came from saying yes to things that at first glance didn't seem to fit into who I was or my preexisting plan. I didn't plan on being a podcaster when I got my PhD—the internet didn't exist. When the filmmaker John Papola emailed me out of the blue and said he wanted to work with me on a project because he liked my podcast, I thought we'd make some kind of video together but neither of us expected to create two rap videos.

Some of the most unforgettable conversations I've had in my life came when I was just there to listen, when I was able to see myself as something other than the star of the story. I didn't have a plan on what I was going to accomplish in the conversation, I was just present when a stranger opened her heart to me about a tragedy in her life. It doesn't happen often, but it's a powerful and precious skill, the ability to be present without judgment.

Instead of entering a conversation with a fundamentally transactional plan—What can I get out of this?—the "star of the story" mindset, approach conversations more like an artist. Avoid having a set of goals. Rather than planning on steering the conversation, let it take its own path. The best conversations go in unexpected directions and end up in places of intimacy, revelation, or education. The conversation, like a work of art, takes on a life of its own. You give up some control and in return the heart opens.

Living like an artist doesn't mean you never plan or that you sit around and wait for life to sweep you off your feet. It means appreciating that how you interact with your experiences has a life of its own.

We all know that we can't really plan our life the way a tourist with the best guidebooks plans an itinerary. If we think of it that way, we have to concede that we live in a kingdom where the trains don't run on time and sometimes don't run at all—a place where the trains make unscheduled stops and often go off the rails and do their own thing despite our best efforts.

But the point isn't "prepared to be surprised." Of course loved ones die, we don't get the job we thought was going to be ours for the taking, our proposal gets rejected. Strangers turn into good friends. Sometimes our ship comes in. Life is full of surprises—nothing new there. What I'm talking about is how we might confront those surprises, setbacks, unexpected gifts, the things that fall into our lap, the things that sweep us off our feet.

Another way to think about life as an artist comes from the act of writing. In theory, it's possible to carefully craft each sentence, and the best writer is the one who patiently finds just the right word and spins sentence after sentence in a beautiful web. I once thought that was the way Flaubert wrote, for example—that his first draft was basically his final draft. But it's not true. Flaubert was a relentless reviser, doing draft after draft until he was satisfied.

When science fiction author Orson Scott Card teaches creative writing, he has the students give one another feedback on their drafts. But instead of grading the students based on their final essays, he grades them on the quality of the feedback they gave their classmates. His insight was that becoming a great writer requires becoming a great editor—learning to revise is essential to writing well. That's true of life, too. Don't worry about the rough draft. As long as you're able to kill your darlings and take advantage of optionality, you will thrive.

The last way to exploit the idea of living like an artist is to see yourself as the work of art, the economist James

Buchanan's "artifactual man" from chapter 9, the idea of seeing yourself as an artifact. Imagine living like an artist where you and your life are the art. What would that mean? It would mean you see yourself as the clay to be molded, the marble to be sculpted. It means to see yourself and your life as a work in progress.

Life is like a book that you are writing and reading at the same time. You might have a plan for how it turns out. But for it to be a great book, it needs to be savored and chewed and digested along the way, like a book you read that changes your life. And you have to prepare for a plot twist and maybe two or three.

You might imagine you can script a book or a poem or your life and have it come out the way you plan. You might even be able to write that script and execute that plan. But the lesson of the first half of this book is that the book you want to inhabit when you're a teenager or in your twenties may not be the best book for you as you get older. You need to let the book have its own way with you.

This perspective requires a level of self-awareness that usually comes with age and experience. It requires a level of aspiration I wrote about earlier—of thinking about what you want to become at least in general, even if you don't know the precise shape or outline of what you are striving toward. It might simply be "better"—to be a better person this year than last year.

The artist comes into the world with a set of skills. We all do. How are we to use those skills? What are we to fashion from those skills? How can we enhance those skills so as to make even better art out of our lives? How do we take the soil we find ourselves in and transform what we begin with to make it into something beautiful, a work of art?

The movie *Babette's Feast* is the story of an unlikely artist—a maid to a pair of unmarried sisters striving to keep their father's legacy alive in a tiny and dwindling religious community. Babette, the maid, has a windfall and decides to give her employers and their meager flock a night to remember—a meal of extraordinary artistry and craft. One of the characters, after experiencing Babette's creations, remarks: "Through all the world there goes one long cry from the heart of the artist—give me leave to do my utmost." It is not a bad way to think of life and what our hearts long to tell us. We have skills: some given to us, some we earn through effort. We should use those gifts and the precious time allotted to us to the utmost.

The challenge is that we too often think that doing one's

utmost is about racing around at full speed toward a goal. A story is told of Rabbi Levi Yitzchak of Berditchev coming upon a man running, frantically rushing forward. Where are you headed in such a hurry? the rabbi asked. I'm chasing my livelihood! the man answered. Maybe it is behind you, the rabbi said, and you're heading away from it.

There are actually some fine guidebooks to help you plan your trip to Rome. You can build a tight, precise itinerary, the whole trip choreographed to see what you decide in advance is the best. A different type of tourist leaves time to see what happens, what catches one's fancy. There's a tenor on the street pouring his heart out singing Puccini's "Nessun dorma." Some tourists stay longer at the Vatican than they expected. They linger on that bridge over the Tiber and try to imagine how long people have stood at that spot.

Living well is a mix of both of these approaches. That's obvious, but for some reason, we think of the tourist who has planned out the entire trip as rational and the tourist who builds in time for "nothing," the flaneur just taking in the city, as "aimless." Sometimes being aimless helps you discover where to aim.

Sometimes it's better to sit and wait and watch and

see what happens. Sometimes doing your utmost means merely waiting. But it's not waiting idly. It's waiting attentively. It's about paying attention. Sometimes doing your utmost means doing nothing but being ready for what comes next. Slowing down can help you see it, when it arrives.

12

Summing Up

If you live in Washington, DC, and you want to drive to Chicago as quickly as possible, it's not enough to consult the sun or the stars and point your car to the northwest. You need to chart a path. In the old days, you did that with a map. Today, you use Waze or Google Maps to get where you want to go.

The essence of Waze or any navigation program is the turn-by-turn directions. The alternative—making random turns based on intuition—is the road to nowhere. Data is the secret sauce that makes Waze work: data about the system of roads and their characteristics, but also data on

Data

the traffic. Knowing the speed of the traffic on different routes allows Waze to help me get where I want to go more quickly.

A 3x3 Rubik's Cube has forty-three quintillion combinations. That's a forty-three with eighteen zeros after it. Turning a Rubik's Cube randomly is not very likely to lead to a solution. You need a plan, an algorithm—which is just a fancy word for a series of actions or procedures that logically produce a particular outcome.

It's tempting to think of Waze or a Rubik's Cube as a metaphor for life. If we want to achieve our goals, we need a plan to get there from here, an algorithm, a plan based on the best data and information that's available. The better the data, the better the plan, the more we can achieve.

But that only works for tame problems. For wild problems we need a different approach. We need to think about not just the best route, but where to go in the first place. Instead of seeing life as a series of decision nodes where you maximize happiness or well-being looking ahead as best you can, I've suggested that you see it instead as a journey.

Should I take company—a lover or a friend or friends—and if so, who should I ask to come with me? On that journey, how should I treat my fellow travelers? How might I experience the trip if I try to find an itinerary that emerges from our shared vision and not just what makes me the happiest? What principles should I use and how might I implement them on the journey? How do I make room for serendipity, the unexpected and the unavoidable reality that the unexpected is to be expected? Do I have the courage to let the path emerge and unfold? Do I have the courage to let my self, my essence, and how I live and love emerge and unfold as well, as something organic rather than mechanical?

These questions don't have answers. They're not problems to be solved but mysteries to be experienced, tasted, and savored. There are more things in heaven and earth than are dreamt of not just in your philosophy but in what you might expect down the road as you go through life. Life isn't Wazeable. In the meantime, you can continue to work on yourself as an artifact you craft.

Our natural impulse is to ask: What's in it for me? Will I enjoy this? Is this going to be fun? In many parts of life, that's not a bad starting place. For wild problems, seek instead a life well lived, and what is in it for you may turn out to be more than you could have planned or hoped for in advance. Happiness, at least in the sense of stuff that's fun and makes you feel good, is overrated. It can't be reduced to a numerical answer on a scale of 1 to 5 in response to a survey question. It isn't a good thing for humans, or policymakers, to aim for. Meaning, purpose, love, flourishing, using our gifts to the fullest, these are what make our hearts sing. They raise us up to something greater than ourselves.

When I argue that there are parts of life outside the reach of science or the scientific method, I'm sometimes called irrational or anti-science. But using science where it belongs and not using it where it does not belong is the essence of good science. Recognizing the limitations of science and where it applies is a virtue—a sign of healthy humility. There are things we do not know. There may even be things we will never know. But much of the best that we experience in life is not something we know or don't know. The best questions are the ones without answers.

In the final strip of the *Calvin and Hobbes* comic, Bill Watterson, the artist, showed Calvin, a six-year-old boy, tobogganing joyously down a hill freshly covered with pristine snow alongside his stuffed tiger, Hobbes. Calvin tells Hobbes it's a day full of possibilities. Then he says, "It's a magical world, Hobbes, ol' buddy . . . Let's go exploring!"

The exploring is part of what makes the world so magical. Over the years, as I've experienced life, I've become less of an economist and more of a Calvin-ist. The importance of exploring is a way of understanding that you are a work in progress. You need to give some thought to where you want to go and who you will be when you get there. Here's my poetic advice for the journey. Let's call it "Travel Advisory."

Beware the urge for certainty.
The mortal lock.
The sure thing.
The lure of the bird in the hand.

Maybe once or twice, put all your eggs in one basket.
Take a chance
On romance. Ask her out. Or him.
Embrace doubt.
Go out on a limb.

Leave the safety of the streetlight.
Leave the comfort of the campfire.
Delight in the night.
Without being a vampire.

Find company.
Make friends, amends.
The star? Try being one of the cast.
Go far, not fast.

Stretch. Reach.
Sometimes go for the highest hanging peach.

Don't run. Walk.
Sometimes wait and watch.
Try smoky scotch. Not nice? Try it twice.
Or thrice.
For principles, ignore the price.

Don't cower.
Flower,
Flourish.
Nourish
Your inner fire.
Aspire.
Aim high. Better still—aim higher.

I wish you a life well lived, with time in the pool and time away from the pool, doing things that are meaningful to you and meaningful to those who are at your side. Safe travels.

Acknowledgments

Writing a book is a lot like taking a trip to Rome. I was lucky to have a number of special companions along for the ride. I am grateful to my editor at Portfolio/Penguin, Bria Sandford, for her optimism, insight, and devotion to making this book greater than I could make it on my own. My conversations with her, along with her specific suggestions for making it better, had a huge impact on what you've read here. I want to thank my agent, Rafe Sagalyn, who kept me focused, as he always does, on what the book is about. Maureen Clark did a superb job with copyediting, with excellent proofreading assistance from Mike

Brown and Katy Miller. They, along with Randee Marullo, discovered and fixed many of my writing tics, and by doing so made this book a more pleasing read.

I want to thank Jonathan Baron, Don Boudreaux, Agnes Callard, Ben Casnocha, Tyler Cowen, Yuval Dolev, Angela Duckworth, Carolyn Duede, Phoebe Ellsworth, Shalom Freedman, Julia Galef, Lisa Harris, Avi Hofman, Rebekah Iliff, Dan Klein, Arnold Kling, Moshe Koppel, Barbara Kupfer, Lauren Landsburg, Penny Lane, Richard Mahoney, Robert McDonald, Michael Munger, Emily Oster, Niki Papadopoulos, Azra Raza, Aryeh Roberts, Ezra Roberts, Joe Roberts, Shirley Roberts, Yael Roberts, Zev Roberts, Bevis Schock, Hyim Shafner, Spencer Smith, Rob Wiblin, and Shawn Wood for moral support, helpful comments, or conversations about wild problems or reactions to various drafts.

A. J. Jacobs set me in a good direction early on and had many helpful suggestions. Gary Belsky, as always, gave me relentlessly good advice and crucial insight from start to finish. His knowledge of the literature on decision-making was particularly helpful. His confidence in the project sustained me through some tough stretches. My new colleagues at Shalem College, Leon Kass and Dan

194

Polisar, helped me find my way when *Wild Problems* was the wildest of problems. Leon reminded me of what flourishing is really about. I am especially grateful to Dan for numerous valuable line edits and for helping me restructure the manuscript successfully at a critical juncture. A conversation with Zev Roberts helped me find the key to unlocking the structure of the last part of the book.

I want to thank Dan Gilbert for sharing his unpublished "Three Views of Water: Some Reflections on a Lecture by Daniel Kahneman," as well as for a very provocative email correspondence about the pig versus the philosopher. While he agreed that I had represented him fairly in the discussion here, he remains unconvinced of my argument, which in its own peculiar way makes me happy. I want to thank Paul Bloom for alerting me to Gilbert's views.

I am grateful to Julia Galef for a provocative and civil back-and-forth about the value of happiness surveys in helping people to decide whether to become parents. Our conversation at Pairagraph taught me something and sharpened my own perspective.

I want to thank my Twitter follower Nate Wilcox, who asked the question that I used in chapter 1, which helped me think about what this book is about: "If the important things are hard to measure, and the measurable things misleading, what kind of decision framework is left?"

Thanks to the support of Liberty Fund, I have been able to host my weekly podcast, *EconTalk*, for sixteen years. This has allowed me to ask very smart and interesting people questions about things that interest me. In recent years, I've become interested in the life well led, the value of happiness research, how we find meaning, the limits of economics in assessing well-being, and many other topics related to this book.

In many ways, this book grew out of conversations with the following *EconTalk* guests: Michael Blastland, Paul Bloom, Robert Burton, Lorne Buchman, Agnes Callard, Luca Dellanna, David Deppner, Richard Epstein, Julia Galef, Gerd Gigerenzer, Roya Hakakian, Daniel Haybron, Margaret Heffernan, Leon Kass, John Kay, Mervyn King, Dan Klein, Iain McGilchrist, Jerry Muller, Michael Munger, Scott Newstok, L. A. Paul, Richard Robb, Emiliana Simon-Thomas, Peter Singer, Rory Sutherland, and Nassim Nicholas Taleb. You can find these episodes organized at russroberts.info/wildproblems.

Many of these conversations and the books they were

based on affected my thinking in ways I can no longer disentangle from my own thoughts. These *EconTalk* guests surely do not agree with everything here; some would disagree strongly with what I've written. But they all taught me something, even if I can't always point reliably to what that was exactly. If I unconsciously used your ideas, my *EconTalk* guests, please forgive me.

I am grateful to Stripe and Nikki Finnemann for the opportunity to present some of my earliest thoughts on the challenge of making analytical decisions using data.

And as with all my books, I couldn't have gotten here without the counsel, comments, and support of my wife, Sharon. Together, we have made many leaps into the darkness, far from the streetlight. What a blessing it has been to have her at my side.

Sources and Further Reading

Two books and one article were central to my thinking as I charted this book's course; all three are very much worth reading: *Aspiration* by Agnes Callard; *Transformative Experience* by L. A. Paul; and "Big Decisions: Opting, Converting, Drifting" by Edna Ullmann-Margalit, in the *Royal Institute of Philosophy Supplement* 58 (2006): 157–72. The *EconTalk* interviews I did with Callard and Paul about their books were very helpful. Paul's concept of the vampire problem got me to think about rationality in a whole new light.

Lord Kelvin said, "When you can measure what you are speaking about, and express it in numbers, you know something about it; but when you cannot measure it, when you cannot express it in numbers, your knowledge is of a meagre and unsatisfactory kind: it may be the beginning of knowledge, but you have scarcely, in your thoughts, advanced to the stage of *science*, whatever the matter may be." The quote is from *Popular Lectures and Addresses*, vol. 1 (1889), "Electrical Units of Measurement," delivered May 3, 1883.

What is carved into stone at the University of Chicago is a paraphrase: "When you cannot measure, your knowledge is meager and unsatisfactory." In 1959, Vernon Smith was invited by George Stigler to present a paper at the University of Chicago. Both men would go on to win the Nobel Prize in economics. Smith tells the story that when they came upon the quote, Stigler quipped: "And when you *can* measure, your knowledge is meager and unsatisfactory!" Stigler was a very witty and very empirical economist, but I like to think his joke was a reference to the limits of data in fully understanding the world.

I first learned of Darwin's deliberations about marriage years ago in *Wing to Wing, Oar to Oar: Readings on*

Courting and Marrying, the wonderful collection of readings on love edited by Amy and Leon Kass. Agnes Callard's essay in the *Boston Review* titled "Don't Overthink It" sent me back to Darwin's dilemma and got me thinking about decision-making as this book was being born. A. J. Jacobs's *Esquire* essay titled "Charles Darwin and How to Fix Valentine's Day" also gave me insights into Darwin, and much amusement.

Useful background on Darwin and his marital journey came from his autobiography, which can be found on the website Darwin Online (darwin-online.org.uk)—you can view Darwin's handwritten journal entry by searching for "CUL-DAR210.8.2"—and from the Darwin Correspondence Project (darwinproject.ac.uk). Data on his *Beagle* voyage came from the *Britannica* article about the trip: britannica.com/biography/Charles-Darwin/The-Beagle -voyage.

Background on Francis Bacon came from Daphne du Maurier's book *The Winding Stair* and John Henry's book *Knowledge Is Power*.

Using an index of attributes for hiring a job candidate is described in *Thinking, Fast and Slow* by Daniel Kahneman. The quote from Elizabeth Stone that to decide to have a child is to "decide forever to have your heart go walking around outside your body" was quoted without attribution in a 1985 *Village Voice* essay by Ellen Cantarow. *Reader's Digest* reprinted the quote in 1987 and verified that Cantarow was quoting Elizabeth Stone. I thank Elizabeth Stone for confirming this history via personal email.

The quotes from Persi Diaconis come from a speech that was reprinted under the title "The Problem of Thinking Too Much" (statweb.stanford.edu/~cgates/PERSI/papers/thinking.pdf).

The starting point of this book is that we have some control over our decision-making and can conceive of making a rational choice. Luca Dellanna's book *The Control Heuristic* explores the ways our brain makes this difficult and ways that we might gain a little more control.

The John Stuart Mill quote about the pig and the philosopher comes from his book *Utilitarianism*.

Paul Bloom's book *The Sweet Spot* reminded me that suffering has its virtues and that we don't care only about how much suffering we experience relative to pleasure—the order in which we experience the suffering and the pleasure also matters.

I cannot remember where I read the story of the student who must bring the stone to the top of the tower. If you know the source, please email me at russroberts@gmail .com.

Roger Scruton's book *Where We Are* and my *EconTalk* interview with Megan McArdle about the book helped me think about the centrality of place in our identity.

For more on Adam Smith and *The Theory of Moral Sentiments*, see my book *How Adam Smith Can Change Your Life: An Unexpected Guide to Human Nature and Happiness.*

For a more serious and powerful look at Penelope's Problem, read Amy Kass's essay "The Homecoming of Penelope," in *Apples of Gold in Pictures of Silver: Honoring the Work of Leon R. Kass.*

Thomas Ferguson's "Who Solved the Secretary Problem?," from *Statistic Science* 4, no. 3 (August, 1989): 282–89, available at jstor.org/stable/2245639, is an excellent and amusing introduction to Martin Gardner's challenge in *Scientific American*. It includes a fabulous description of how the astronomer Johannes Kepler spent two years systematically working through eleven potential marriage partners after his wife died of cholera. Kepler's anguished attempt to "rationally" choose his next wife is a fine illustration of the themes of this book.

My appreciation of the importance of weaving a shroud grew out of my *EconTalk* conversation with Virginia Postrel about her book *The Fabric of Civilization: How Textiles Made the World.*

The Wikipedia entry on "Satisficing" is an accessible introduction to Herbert Simon's alternative perspective to optimizing. Braver readers can tackle Simon's article that introduced the term, "Rational Choice and the Structure of the Environment," in *Psychological Review* 63, no. 2 (1956): 129–38.

The Chesterton Fence can be found in G. K. Chesterton's book *The Thing.*

Chapter 8 is adapted from my essay "The Story of My Life" at https://link.medium.com/M6E1ze00ppb.

Rabbi Jonathan Sacks wrote about contracts versus covenants in his essay "The Bonds of Love," available at rabbisacks.org.

Ariel Rubinstein's view of rational decision-making comes from the opening pages of his book *Economic Fables.*

Harry Frankfurt's insights into our desires about our desires come from his 1971 *Journal of Philosophy* essay, "Freedom of the Will and the Concept of a Person." I explore our desires about our desires in my *Medium* essay "Wanting to Want What We Want." The Frank Knight quote about habit formation is from "The Planful Act: The Possibilities and Limitations of Collective Rationality," in *Freedom and Reform: Essays in Economics and Social Philosophy.* The Knight quote about humans as aspiring, not desiring, beings comes from "Ethics and the Economic Interpretations," *Quarterly Journal of Economics* 36 (May 1922): 454–81. The James Buchanan quote about seeing yourself as something to be crafted is from "Natural and Artifactual Man," in *What Should Economists Do?*

The Eliot Rosen version of the two dogs story (sometimes told about two wolves) comes from his 1998 book, *Experiencing the Soul.*

My speculations about Bill Belichick's draft strategy come from my observations over the years, seeing how he drafts and uses the preseason to create a roster for the regular season.

The quote from Rabbi Jonathan Sacks about the challenge of knowing something until we've done it comes from his essay "Doing and Hearing" at rabbisacks.org.

The William Faulkner quote about following your characters around and writing down what they say and do comes from his 1958 visit to a University of Virginia graduate class (faulkner.lib.virginia.edu/display/wfaudio21).

My understanding of Flaubert as an inveterate reviser comes from the appropriately titled "Writing as Thinking," by Keith Oatley and Maja Djikic, *Review of General Psychology* (March 2008).

Elizabeth Bishop's poem "One Art" is widely available on the internet, along with many powerful interpretations. Try "One Art: The Writing of Loss in Elizabeth Bishop's Poetry" by the blogger Beth at *Bluedragonfly10*, which I referenced in chapter 11 (bluedragonfly10.wordpress.com /2009/06/12/one-art-the-writing-of-loss-in-elizabeth -bishop's-poetry), and "19 Lines That Turn Anguish into Art" by Dwight Garner and Parul Sehgal (nytimes.com /interactive/2021/06/18/books/elizabeth-bishop-one-art -poem.html).

Orson Scott Card's insight into the importance of editing when learning to write came from a personal conversation we had when I gave a talk at Southern Virginia University. He kindly shared advice for my course on writing and communication for economics graduate students.